Mark Oakley is Dean of St John's College, Cambridge, and is a Visiting Lecturer in the Department of Theology and Religious Studies, King's College London. He was formerly Canon Chancellor of St Paul's Cathedral, overseeing the arts and learning programmes. Mark writes regularly for the *Church Times* and *The Tablet* and broadcasts frequently on BBC Radio 4. His latest bestselling book *The Splash of Words: Believing in poetry* (Canterbury Press, 2016) was published to great acclaim. He's also the editor of *A Good Year, Readings for Funerals* and *Readings for Weddings* (SPCK, 2016, 2015 and 2013 respectively). In 2019, he won the Michael Ramsey Prize for theological writing.

MY SOUR-SWEET DAYS

George Herbert and the journey of the soul

Mark Oakley

First published in Great Britain in 2019

Society for Promoting Christian Knowledge
36 Causton Street
London SW1P 4ST
www.spck.org.uk

British Library Cataloguing-in-Publication Data
A catalogue record for this book is available from the British Library

ISBN 978–0–281–08032–8
eBook ISBN 978–0–281–08033–5

Typeset by Manila Typesetting Company
First printed in Great Britain by Ashford Colour Press
Subsequently digitally reprinted in Great Britain

eBook by Manila Typesetting Company

Produced on paper from sustainable forests

To

Deborah Stuart

a loving and constant friend

I will complain, yet praise;
I will bewail, approve:
And all my sowre-sweet days
I will lament, and love.
(George Herbert, 'Bitter-sweet')

God will bring us to heaven, but it must be by hell. God will bring us to comfort, but it must be by sense of our own un-worthiness. He will forgive our sins, but it must be by sight and sense of our sins. He will bring us to life, but it must be by death. He will bring us to glory, but it must be by shame. God works by contraries; therefore in contraries believe contraries. (Richard Sibbes)

Contents

Contents

Preface

My God must have my best, ev'n all I had.

'Lead us not into interpretation' must be the prayer of anyone wishing to introduce a poet's work to those who may be unfamiliar with it. I've tried to say it daily as I've put together this short collection of some of George Herbert's poems. My brief reflections try to clarify words we may not use today or help with some reference that may not be immediately clear. I've inevitably added a few thoughts of my own en route but in the hope that they will entice readers to do their own reading of the poems and to encounter their most extraordinary author. I have tried to keep each reflection of such a length that a busy life might just about find the time to get through one a day.

George Herbert (1593–1633) is a poet worth getting to know for anyone interested in humanity's inner being, the benefits of honesty, the mystery and love of God and what can be made of religion in a world of projections. For those who wish to learn more about the man's life, the fascinating historical period he lived through and how his poems can be intelligently read nearly four hundred years later, I can do no better than recommend you read Dr John Drury's biography of Herbert, *Music at Midnight: The life and poetry of George Herbert* (2013). For those who want to excavate more deeply into Herbert's literary skills, ingenuities (nearly every one of his poems has a different form) and use of language, while remaining sympathetic to the seasons of his soul, anything written by Professor Helen Wilcox will prove more than rewarding.

There has sometimes been debate as to whether Herbert is a major minor poet or a minor major poet. It's a debate that doesn't get us very far. What is clear is that he is a loved poet and that, as Richard Baxter wrote in 1681 (A7v), 'Herbert speaks to God like one that really believeth in God . . . Heart-work and Heaven-work make up his Books.'

All Herbert's poems, in one way or another, are about God. They are all deeply in tune with the human heart and the agitated human mind (he refers to his thoughts as a 'case of knives' at one point, in 'Affliction (IV)'). It has made him appeal to people of faith and none across every spectrum. Charles I read Herbert in prison and Oliver Cromwell's chaplain recommended him to his friends. Samuel Taylor Coleridge (1887, pp. 248–9) said Herbert helped him with his 'tendency to self-contempt'. Like the parables of Jesus, they often do their work using images of day-to-day life and in a familiar voice, but this recognized world is infused with, wrestles and dances with, that other world for which religious faith desires and which prayer seeks to find a path to.

I think that one of Herbert's lasting influences on me is his insistence that God is the loving friend of human beings and not some distant, overbearing tyrant. God is the one who takes Herbert's hand smiling. Salvation for Herbert is the cure for our self-observant perfectionism, that noise within which creates such chaos around us. Hell is hardly mentioned in the poetry. Herbert knows that he is secure within the love of his friend and nothing will ever get in their way. What I love about Herbert is that this belief in God as friend means he doesn't put God on some pious pedestal but talks to him – often bantering with or berating him for the painful failures and hardness of our feeling life or, sometimes, of the Christian life. He also looks at himself and how he treats his friend and concludes in one poem 'use I not my foes, as I use Thee'. The great poetry critic Professor Helen Vendler has referred to Herbert's 'startling accomplishment in revising the conventional vertical address to God until it approaches the horizontal address to an intimate friend' (2005, p. 9). If a friend is the one in whom all our loose ends find a home, then God is the friend of George Herbert.

There is an audacious boldness, unflinching honesty about good and bad, and a disarming playfulness in Herbert's conversation with God. This is a beautiful, faithful antidote to the cold and tortured talk of God in some churches today and a corrective to the warm shallows of those who talk about God as if God were akin to yoga or basket-weaving, something you take up on a Wednesday evening for self-improvement. If you regret the fact that Christianity today so often appears to be a choice between ignorance on fire and intelligence on ice, then Herbert is for you, embodying as he does a critical and loving fidelity. God for Herbert is not an object we fuss over and fall out over, but the subject to whom my life must relate most seriously and deeply. God is never the object of our knowledge for him. God is the generous cause of our wonder.

I hope as you read these 40 poems from his *The Temple* that you discover you like Herbert the person. It was W. H. Auden who wrote, 'I think that any reader of his poetry will conclude that George Herbert must have been an exceptionally good man, and exceptionally nice as well' (1973, p. 7). I hope you will be grateful to him for opening his soul to us as a mirror in which we can recognize ourselves and learn more about the love that he knew is always seeking to find us beyond the mirror, in the heart. God is always anticipatory in the poems, a few steps ahead of Herbert, and waiting for him to catch up so they can have a rest together. Many of the poems are psalm-like, love poems even, and speak for us in every mood and complexity. One gets the sense that Herbert's poetic formality set the boundaries for an often raw, often tender spirit. He was a person at some peace with his lack of peace, whose faith was an anchor that occasionally dislodged but kept him, nevertheless, in harbour.

Isaak Walton, whose biography of Herbert is great to read, but may be historically questionable in parts, says that as Herbert reached the end of his life, aged only 40 and having been ordained for only three years, he packaged up his as yet unpublished poems and sent them to his friend Nicholas Ferrar at Little Gidding. If Ferrar thought the poems were any good, then he left them to him, but if not he could put them on the fire. Ferrar kept well away from the hearth, thank goodness. Herbert had talked of his 'poore silly soul' (in 'Vanitie (II)') and these poems, he wrote to Ferrar, were about 'the many spiritual conflicts that have passed betwixt God and my soul, before I could subject mine to the will of Jesus my Master, in whose service I have now found perfect freedom' (Walton, 1670/1995, p. 380).

George Herbert is a good companion with whom to examine the journey of our own soul. We read him and wonder which compass we have picked up in life and where it is ultimately pointing us. His poems are indeed heart-work and heaven-work.

Mark Oakley
Cambridge, 2019

The Agonie

Philosophers have measur'd mountains
Fathom'd the depths of seas, of states, and kings,
Walk'd with a staffe to heav'n, and traced fountains:
  But there are two vast, spacious things,
The which to measure it doth more behove:
Yet few there are that sound them; Sinne and Love.

Who would know Sinne, let him repair
Unto mount Olivet; there shall he see
A man so wrung with pains, that all his hair,
  His skinne, his garments bloudie be.
Sinne is that presse and vice, which forceth pain
To hunt his cruell food through ev'ry vein.

Who knows not Love, let him assay
And taste that juice, which on the crosse a pike
Did set again abroach; then let him say
  If ever he did taste the like.
Love is that liquour sweet and most divine,
Which my God feels as bloud; but I, as wine.

It often takes some crisis in life to make us come to our senses
and to understand, at last, the things that really matter. Herbert
begins this poem commenting that the greatest thinkers in
our world have applied themselves to physical and political

sciences in a search to fathom life. A *staffe* is a measuring rod that astrologers used to get some insight from the stars. Herbert uses the idea of people measuring the world twice in the first verse and alerts us to the foolishness in thinking that measuring the world alone somehow gets the 'measure' of reality. Instead, says Herbert, we should be reflecting on *two vast, spacious things*. These are *Sinne* and *Love*, the things that limit the self and the things that expand it. These are the unignorable forces in life that build relationships or destroy them. Strangely, he adds, few *sound* them – that is, dive into their depths.

Herbert then points us in the right direction if we want to learn more about sin and love. In fact, we must travel in the same direction to understand both. We must go to the Mount of Olives, where we find Christ in agony before his arrest, and then to Golgotha, where Christ is executed. The title of the poem tells us that these are the destinations where sin and love meet, revealing themselves for what they are. The second verse takes up the imagery of the prophet Isaiah (63.1–3), where we hear of a man whose clothes are stained red: 'I have trodden the winepress alone; and of the people there was none with me.' In medieval days, the image of the winepress was often used to symbolize Christ's suffering and Herbert takes up the theme. Christ is *wrung* with injury and sin is that *presse and vice* (a pun with the word 'vice' is surely intended) that brings such pain to a person suffering its murderous hatred. A press extracts the juice from fruits by means of pressure, crushing them. In a dark and ominous image, the agony Christ suffers is sin hunting his *cruell food* through all his body and *through ev'ry vein*.

Herbert in the second verse addresses those who would know *Sinne* and asks them to look. There needs to be a clear recognition of what sin is and what it can do. In the third verse, however, he speaks to the one *who knows not Love* and this time he doesn't ask us to see but to taste – that is, to experience it. Love can be understood only by being loved and by loving. It has been noted that this poem begins with lovers of knowledge and ends with knowers of love. This happens because Herbert invites us to partake in the juice from the press of love. With St John's account of the piercing of Christ's side in view (John 19.34), he refers to those who *set . . . abroach*, which is the act of pushing a hole into a wine cask for pouring. He ends with a startling couplet, an imaginative reversal of the doctrine that in the Eucharist wine becomes the blood of Christ. Here, his blood becomes wine and we are drawn into a grateful and graceful sharing of it. Knowing we are so loved, we experience a joy that comes from, and not despite, a full and shared knowledge in God of the cost of our freedom and choice. This is a poem that celebrates the magnitude and endless outpouring of God's love. Trying to stop God loving us is as impossible as trying to stop a pierced wine cask from letting its matured beauty flow out for our pleasure and sustenance.

We noticed at the beginning that Herbert refers to us measuring life. Sin has often been understood as what happens when good things are taken to excess. To eat is good, but gluttony isn't. To have a healthy sense of self-worth is good, but vanity curdles it – and so on. In other words, life is best lived in a balance and we need to measure ourselves carefully and in the perspective of eternity to strike this balance well. The balance will always be helped by love and tilted badly through selfishness. If only, urges Herbert, the great minds of our day gave more time to understanding such things.

Redemption

Having been tenant long to a rich Lord,
    Not thriving, I resolved to be bold,
    And make a suit unto him, to afford
A new small-rented lease, and cancell th' old.

In heaven at his manour I him sought:
    They told me there, that he was lately gone
    About some land, which he had dearly bought
Long since on earth, to take possession.

I straight return'd, and knowing his great birth,
    Sought him accordingly in great resorts;
    In cities, theatres, gardens, parks, and courts:
At length I heard a ragged noise and mirth

    Of theeves and murderers: there I him espied,
    Who straight, *Your suit is granted*, said, & died.

Redemption is the process by which land that has been mort-
gaged or pledged is bought back or reclaimed. This is usually
achieved through payment of the debt owed. Using this image
of clearing a liability, Herbert writes a sonnet that, in Louis
MacNeice's words, is 'an allegory in miniature' (1965, p. 8). It
has a natural tone that, aligned with a recognizable everyday
landscape, reminds us of a parable. It ends with what has been

called 'one of the most sheerly exciting lines in all religious poetry' (Nuttall, 1980, p. 34).

The poet says that he has been a tenant to a *rich Lord* for a long time but, during that time, he has not been *thriving*. He takes a deep breath and decides to be bold. He resolves to go and make a *suit*, petitioning his landlord to improve his situation by giving him (*afford*) a less costly deal and cancelling their former agreement.

Although we are told that the lord's *manour* is in *heaven*, the poem maintains its everyday feel. The poet gets there and is told that the lord has lately gone to *some land*, which he *had dearly bought . . . to take possession*. The speaker immediately sets about finding him in *great resorts*, places where large numbers of fashionable people gather together. Eventually, though, he hears a harsh or *ragged noise* mingled with some amusement of *theeves and murderers*. At this point we realize that his landlord is the victim and we are at Calvary, where two thieves were crucified beside Jesus and soldiers played dice, taunting him as he hung suspended there. The poet sees Jesus and, before he can do or say anything, the Lord speaks to him, telling him that *Your suit is granted*; the new covenant is agreed to; and then, as soon as it is spoken, Jesus dies. The last line has a rather cumbersome feel to it, but it leads us to the last word *died* having a noticeable force.

Many commentators believe this poem to be about the juncture of the Old and New Covenants with God, how one is fulfilled by the other with a free and loving grace. For others, it is a work that shows how we are all incapable of earning God's love, and even though we can seek God out, hoping we can make a good deal with him, the love he gives, the love which is faithful to us and allows us to be free and at home in God, is lavished on us without any cost. It is also a poem that reminds us where in the world to seek the true God and not the God of our own imagining who so naturally approves of our style and modish lives. So often we need to be redeemed not just from our belongings but also from who we have become.

Is this also a poem about wanting to change your life? Is it about recognizing the point when your life is not thriving and you need a new contract? The ego is the part of us that loves the status quo, even when it isn't working, and attaches our identity to the past and present, fearing the future. The speaker looks for the God of transformation in all his own haunts, but needs to go outside the wall to hear words that will change him for ever. They are words of a loving and reckless generosity and they are spoken as God's last.

Easter

Rise heart; thy Lord is risen. Sing his praise
                              Without delayes,
Who takes thee by the hand, that thou likewise
                              With him mayst rise:
That, as his death calcined thee to dust,
His life may make thee gold, and much more just.

Awake, my lute, and struggle for thy part
                              With all thy art.
The crosse taught all wood to resound his name,
                              Who bore the same.
His stretched sinews taught all strings, what key
Is best to celebrate this most high day.

Consort both heart and lute, and twist a song
                              Pleasant and long:
Or since all musick is but three parts vied
                              And multiplied;
O let thy blessed Spirit bear a part,
And make up our defects with his sweet art.

I got me flowers to straw thy way;   _Spiritual pumpkins_ (9)
I got me boughs off many a tree:
But thou wast up by break of day,
And brought'st thy sweets along with thee.

The Sunne arising in the East,
Though he give light, & th' East perfume;
If they should offer to contest
With thy arising, they presume.

Can there be any day but this,
Though many sunnes to shine endeavour?
We count three hundred, but we misse:
There is but one, and that one ever.

Many will know Ralph Vaughan Williams's setting of this poem and, as it contains many musical references this seems appropriate. In fact, there are two poems here, with different metrical patterns, next to one another but under one title. It is generally thought that Psalm 57, the psalm set for Easter Day, was an inspiration to Herbert here: 'Awake up, my glory; awake, lute and harp: I myself will awake right early. I will give thanks unto thee, O Lord, among the people: and I will sing unto thee among the nations' (57.9–10, BCP).

This beautiful poem begins with Herbert addressing his heart. *Rise*, he says to it, because *thy Lord is risen*. Easter was one of the three days in the year when people attended the Communion service, when the priest asks the congregation to 'lift up' their hearts. As in other of Herbert's poems, the Lord takes him *by the hand*, a sign of loving union and friendship, and leads him to share the risen life with him. Christ's death had reduced Herbert's heart to ashes, *calcined*, but now his life will transform it into *gold* and make it justified. *Just* can also mean tuned well, in tune with itself.

Herbert then speaks to his *lute*, urging it to wake up and do all it can to praise the risen Lord. He refers to the *crosse* on which Christ died but, as metaphor, to that cross on a musical instrument where wood and string meet. Like those same strings, Christ's *sinews* were *stretched* (and here there is a pun on the sound of 'taut') to make redeeming music, but they also *taught* all strings how to find the higher key of sacred music of the time to appropriately celebrate his resurrection. The image of Christ's strained body on wood being a stringed instrument is found in other poems, more recently in R. S. Thomas's 'The Musician' (1995, p. 104), where 'it was himself that he played' and God listens.

Herbert's heart and lute are told to *consort* and come together to *twist a song*, twisting into a cord or chord. He then refers to the harmony of music being based on the common chord or triad. To *vie* means to multiply by increase or repetition. He then speaks to God and asks that his blessed Spirit would *bear a part* – that is, play a line in the polyphonic music that will make up what is missing.

There is now a shift in tone. A rather old-fashioned and unrefined use of *I got me* perhaps allows us to see how, in the presence of the risen Lord, we are all, as it were, spiritual bumpkins. All our pretensions and honours, our robes and salaries, count as nothing as we see ourselves, simply, as loved by Love and for always. Herbert gets *flowers* and branches to put on the path of his Lord, with echoes of Palm Sunday. Churches in Herbert's day often placed blossoms and incensed greenery inside to celebrate Easter. Using a morning image, Christ is up before Herbert and has already gathered all that is needed for the day. It has resonances of Christ walking in the morning garden after his resurrection.

The poem recognizes both the glory of the rising sun that pours light on the world and the perfumes from the East that we breathe to feel refreshed. They fall a long way short, continues Herbert, of the light and spice that Christ brings. Christ, as God's sun and son, brings a new light to see by in his rising and, although *many sunnes* try to outshine each other, as do the 'many sons' of Earth, and although there are over *three hundred* sunrises each year, there is now only one day that matters and we live in it now and for ever.

I once saw on a makeshift memorial in the USA, at the site of a police shooting, words written on a box: 'You tried to bury me. You forgot I am a seed.' This came to mind as I read Herbert's poem. The Christ he wants his heart and lute to praise is the Christ who was buried but who now is the seed whose new life grows quietly and unseen in lives that tend the soil of the soul. He is the seed of a new world, for Herbert, and that world, not this one, is where Herbert tried so hard to fix his heart.

Easter Wings

Lord, who createdst man in wealth and store,
Though foolishly he lost the same,
Decaying more and more,
Till he became
Most poore:
With thee
O let me rise
As larks, harmoniously,
And sing this day thy victories:
Then shall the fall further the flight in me.

My tender age in sorrow did beginne:
And still with sicknesses and shame.
Thou didst so punish sinne,
That I became
Most thinne.
With thee
Let me combine,
And feel thy victorie:
For, if I imp my wing on thine,
Affliction shall advance the flight in me.

If you turn this book 90 degrees clockwise, you will see how
the poem is the shape of two sets of wings. The poem was
originally published in 1633 and, as the lines were printed

vertically, readers had to turn the book to be able to read it, but most anthologies today print it as it is here.

As usual, there are biblical passages that without doubt are referenced here. Malachi 4.2 speaks of the Sun of righteousness who will arise 'with healing in his wings' and Isaiah 40.31 confidently asserts that 'they that wait upon the LORD shall renew their strength; they shall mount up with wings as eagles'. These are important because Herbert rarely refers to Christ's life, death or resurrection without also exploring what they mean to his own life. He is consistently pursuing how the words of Scripture find their best translation in his life, words and prayer. The wings are Christ's as he soars in heaven with majestic beauty. They are also Herbert's, feeling their way on the new currents of Christ's risen life.

Herbert prays to God from the first stanza on. God has created us and given us so much but, through the Fall, we lost our real *wealth* – our mutually trusting relationship with God. Our own worst enemies who need to be saved from ourselves, we decay, fall apart and become *poore*. As Herbert writes this, so the stanza thins in the middle, shrinking to accentuate the deterioration and poverty. He prays that he may *rise* like morning birds. He specifically refers to larks, which in Latin are called *alauda* and associated with praise ('laud'), not least because they sing as they rise in flight. He wants to sing, like the birds that greet the sun, of Christ's *victories*.

The last line stands in its own right, almost as a bruised reflection: *Then shall the fall further the flight in me.* The notion that the goodness which came out of the Fall makes the Fall worthwhile is not uncommon. The *felix culpa* motif can be found in writers as diverse as St Augustine, Milton and Richard Rohr, whose book *Falling Upward* (SPCK, 2013) is a contemporary reworking of the theme. Here, the idea is personalized. Herbert can see how his own personal failings and sins have taught him where his compass must now be. As John Donne wrote in his own sickness, 'Therfore that he may raise the Lord throws down' (1952, p. 50).

The second stanza may be read as a description of fallen humanity, born in *sorrow*, with *sicknesses and shame*. It can also be read as autobiographical, as the poet suffered much ill health throughout his life and came to feel ashamed of how he had led such a worldly, proud life that left him very lost. The poem says he became *most thinne* and, again, the form of the stanza pinches in the middle, as the slight humanity he lived, and the impoverished body that somehow speaks of the soul within, lie right in the centre of the verse.

He looks to Christ and asks that they might *combine* so Easter will be a victory he can share in too. Using a term from falconry for when feathers are grafted on to a bird's wing to enable it to fly again, he asks if he can *imp my wing on thine*. He speaks to the one 'with healing in his wings' (Malachi 4.2). The last line shows how the *affliction* that has stopped his flight is now the help he needs in life in order to receive healing and to fly afresh in the strength of his Lord. 'If I take the wings of the morning', prays the psalmist, 'even there shall thy hand lead me' (Psalm 139.9–10).

John Donne wrote a poem to a newly ordained friend and asked him, 'Art thou new feather'd with coelestiall love?' (1952, p. 32). Herbert would have replied 'yes', but only because he had been grounded in life for too long, with too much hurt and despair, and now he is gratefully learning to sing because he is free and to fly because Christ is bearing him up with a love he had never known was possible.

Sinne (I)

Lord, with what care hast thou begirt us round!
    Parents first season us; then schoolmasters
    Deliver us to laws; they send us bound
To rules of reason, holy messengers,

Pulpits and sundayes, sorrow dogging sinne,
    Afflictions sorted, anguish of all sizes,
    Fine nets and stratagems to catch us in,
Bibles laid open, millions of surprises,

Blessings beforehand, tyes of gratefulnesse,
    The sound of glory ringing in our eares:
    Without, our shame; within, our consciences;
Angels and grace, eternall hopes and fears.

    Yet all these fences and their whole aray
    One cunning bosome-sinne blows quite away.

The poet Coleridge admired the 'simple dignity of the language' of this poem (1817/1997, p. xix). It is a sonnet and, though the title may not make us rush to read it, it approaches the subject of sin with the fresh and unexpected perspectives that make Herbert such a good companion. The first letter of John reminds us, 'If we say that we have no sin, we deceive ourselves, and the truth is not in us' (1.8). Much theological work today can either fixate on this fact or avoid it. Herbert always keeps it in the picture but won't allow it to dominate because to say God has a love that won't forgive or help us repair and grow, that only loves some and rejects others, is equally deceiving and untruthful.

Herbert tells God he knows he surrounds us with great *care* from the beginning of our lives in order that we don't fall into ways which harm us or injure others. Sin is what stops us becoming who we are in God's eyes, not living up to the dignity placed there for both our personhood and our potential. Herbert says that parents *first season us*, help us mature, and he was fortunate to have such parents. Schoolteachers then introduce us to moral principles, the wisdom of the past and the *rules of reason* for today.

The poem then catalogues the *holy messengers* God sends, like guardian angels, to keep us in his fold. These include sermons from *pulpits* and *sundayes*, when we gather together to worship and celebrate Christ's resurrection. There are lessons in life that also act as messengers, such as *sorrow dogging sinne*, unhappiness being the consequence of wrongdoing. There are *afflictions* and *anguish* that remind us of our fragility and need of God, as well as other *nets and stratagems to catch us in* – as if we are fish that are liable to swim off into dangerous waters.

Another holy messenger of God's watchfulness is found in *Bibles laid open*, accessible to be read and properly encountered, both questioned and questioning. There are also the *millions of surprises* in life that make us reimagine, change direction or self-scrutinize better. There are moments when the full stops of sin can be changed into the commas of forgiveness, but quite often these happen because we have first ignored the insights given us by the *surprises* of experience and the *blessings* we already have and the promise of those yet to come *ringing in our eares*.

Sinne (I)

The sense of *shame* and the call of conscience, *angels* and those who speak God's truth, *grace* and the deepest hopes and fears that humanity can experience – all these, says Herbert, are the *fences* God encloses us with to guard us from harm. However, *one cunning bosome-sinne*, a sneaky, selfish act that comes from within our darker recesses, can blow the fences down completely. Such is the dangerous banality and the uncontrollable consequence of sin's self-regard. This is a poem which recalls that it is better to do the right thing, even when it's the hard thing.

The last word of the poem is *away*. It makes me think of the prodigal son who goes 'away' into a distant country, propelled by his pride and rejection of home, while his loving dad waits anxiously for his return. For God, each of us is worth far more than the worst thing we have ever done, but Herbert argues that God has given us many signposts to make the journey back much shorter than it might otherwise be.

Affliction (I)

When first thou didst entice to thee my heart,
                I thought the service brave;
So many joyes I writ down for my part,
                Besides what I might have
Out of my stock of naturall delights,
Augmented with thy gracious benefits.

I looked on thy furniture so fine,
                And made it fine to me:
Thy glorious houshold-stuffe did me entwine,
                And 'tice me unto thee.
Such starres I counted mine: both heav'n and earth;
Payd me my wages in a world of mirth.

What pleasures could I want, whose King I served?
                Where joyes my fellows were.
Thus argu'd into hopes, my thoughts reserved
                No place for grief or fear.
Therefore my sudden soul caught at the place,
And made her youth and fierceness seek thy face.

At first thou gav'st me milk and sweetnesses;
                I had my wish and way;
My dayes were straw'd with flow'rs and happinesse;
                There was no moneth but May.

Affliction (I)

But with my yeares sorrow did twist and grow,
And made a partie unawares for wo.

My flesh began unto my soul in pain,
                    Sicknesses cleave my bones;
Consuming agues dwell in ev'ry vein,
                    And tune my breath to grones.
Sorrow was all my soul; I scarce beleeved,
Till grief did tell me roundly, that I lived.

When I got health, thou took'st away my life,
                    And more; for my friends die:
My mirth and edge was lost; a blunted knife
                    Was of more use then I.
Thus thinne and lean without a fence or friend,
I was blown through with ev'ry storm and winde.

Whereas my birth and spirit rather took
                    The way that takes the town;
Thou didst betray me to a lingring book,
                    And wrap me in a gown.
I was entangled in the world of strife,
Before I had the power to change my life.

Yet, for I threatned oft the siege to raise,
                    Not simpring all mine age,
Thou often didst with Academick praise
                    Melt and dissolve my rage.
I took thy sweetned pill, till I came neare;
I could not go away, nor persevere.

Affliction (I)

Yet lest perchance I should too happie be
              In my unhappinesse,
Turning my purge to food, thou throwest me
              Into more sicknesses.
Thus doth thy power crosse-bias me, not making
Thine own gift good, yet me from my wayes taking.

Now I am here, what thou wilt do with me
              None of my books will show.
I reade, and sigh, and wish I were a tree;
              For sure then I should grow
To fruit or shade: at least some bird would trust
Her houshold to me, and I should be just.

Yet, though thou troublest me, I must be meek;
              In weaknesse must be stout.
Well, I will change the service, and go seek
              Some other master out.
Ah my deare God! though I am clean forgot,
Let me not love thee, if I love thee not.

It is thought that Herbert wrote this autobiographical poem sometime in his mid-thirties, before his ordination. It is an extraordinarily honest bit of spiritual stocktaking, often accusatory towards God, and just about held together by the belief Herbert voices in his *A Priest to the Temple, or, The Country Parson* that affliction ultimately is beneficial because it 'softens, and works the stubborn heart of man' (1991, p. 225). One scholar comments that the poem is a remarkable record of 'the achievement of maturity and of the inevitable pains of the process' (Knights, 1946, p. 141).

He begins this prayer poem with what we might think of as the honeymoon with God and life. God entices his *heart*, and he, like someone happy to be serving a friendly new master, finds himself in a good place with *naturall delights* and *gracious benefits*. All the furniture of his faith seemed to fit, although the use of the word *entwine* suggests something of an entanglement that may later prove unhelpful. For now, though, it seemed that heaven and earth *payd me my wages in a world of mirth*. On this wave of a somewhat self-centred happiness, at which he imagines God to be equally delighted, it feels that there was *no moneth but May*; his life felt on the edge of an inevitable warm summertime.

What Herbert couldn't see back then, he says, is that, as time passed, sorrow *did twist and grow*. He is unprepared for when he gets very ill. Only the pain of *grief* reminds him that he is still alive. When he gets better, things get worse: *my friends die*. 'Friends' refers to family members as well as companions. Herbert's two brothers died in their twenties. He loses his edge and thinks that a *blunted knife* is of more use than he is. It's like a hurricane has passed through his soul and left irreparable devastation: *I was blown through with ev'ry storm and winde*.

Herbert continues to look back and recognizes that his class and temperament suited the town's ways and values. Surprisingly, he says that God betrayed him with the books and gowns of university. The use of the words *lingring* and *wrap* bring to mind something deathly. He gets caught up in the world's business before he can do anything about it, becoming someone he'd prefer not to be without even seeing it. When he gets angry at the way life is and how God appears callous, he finds himself lulled by *Academick praise* but his life is in a state of paralysis: *I could not go away, nor persevere*.

Affliction (I)

Just in case Herbert has too many things to be pleased to moan about, he gets sick again and reflects that, at last, the effect of all this affliction is to *crosse-bias* him. This expression meant to be forced to change direction, but it resonates too with the sense of conversion, when our bias is turned towards the cross, the place where suffering is redeemed, and *me from my wayes taking*. But what now? Where is life to go? His books don't help; he reads and sighs and wishes he were *a tree* so that he *should be just*, might be, of some use. *Some bird* might even trust him enough to lay her eggs there. Maybe a dove?

The last verse concludes the poem more than resolves it. It begins as if Herbert has heard the lesson that Paul was taught in 2 Corinthians 12.9: 'My grace is sufficient for you, for power is made perfect in weakness' (NRSV). He knows that he *must be meek*, but then appears to have had enough and wants to find another *master*. There is something about hurt and pain that feels like we are left alone in an empty whitewashed room, forced to see who we really are and what our fears, deep and invisible to us so often, are doing to us. We resent the room and resent even more the one who placed us in it, compelling us to stare at uncomfortable mirrors that demand recognition and change. The last two lines of the poem are famously ambiguous. God is *deare*, both beloved and costly, and Herbert appears to say that now he mustn't claim to love God until he knows more than the honeymoon. The trials and hurts that appear to be written into the contract of life, and the relationship with hope that belief in God asks of us – these are the necessary foundations for any genuine faith to be built on. Only love proves itself worthy of pursuit when life becomes bewildering and disappointing. Herbert has been taught the difference between the intention of love and the reality of it.

21

We live unawakened lives marked by self-perpetuating lies about who we think we are, how we wish to be seen and how God is just like us. Whatever spirituality means today, it implies some assault on this unattractive ego and Herbert, with characteristic honesty, encourages us on our path by telling us a little about his.

Prayer (I)

Prayer the Churches banquet, Angels age,
    Gods breath in man returning to his birth,
    The soul in paraphrase, heart in pilgrimage,
The Christian plummet sounding heav'n and earth;

Engine against th' Almightie, sinners towre,
    Reversed thunder, Christ-side-piercing spear,
    The six-daies world transposing in an houre,
A kinde of tune, which all things heare and fear;

Softnesse, and peace, and joy, and love, and blisse,
    Exalted Manna, gladnesse of the best,
    Heaven in ordinarie, man well drest,
The milkie way, the bird of Paradise,

    Church-bels beyond the starres heard, the souls bloud,
    The land of spices; something understood.

The older I get, the more difficult I find it to describe what
I mean by the word 'prayer'. At the same time, increasingly
I realize how important it is. It's no surprise, then, that I
like this poem. For some it is too frustratingly elusive. It is a
sonnet of metaphors, technically called a 'systrophe', in
which lots of descriptions of something are piled together
without giving an explicit definition. It has no main verb,

which may suggest the timeless relationship of prayer, and demands more than one reading. It appeals, or repels, due to what the poet Louis MacNeice called its 'breathless accumulation of metaphorical images' (1965, p. 46) as it works to capture something of prayer's landscape.

Today when we talk about prayer, we tend to think of something very private and out of view. Herbert, however, launches us straight away into a communal image, a *banquet*, a place where we receive and celebrate shared nourishment. It obviously has eucharistic overtones and recalls Herbert's belief that whereas private prayer is vital, 'where most pray, is heaven' ('The Church-Porch'). Then, in case we think that prayer is something we have made, limited and time-bound, he refers to it as *Angels age* – that is, not trapped within human boundaries but able to reach to the eternal, alert to the transcendent.

We are told in the book of Genesis that Adam was given life by God breathing into him. Here, Herbert says that this breath returns to its birth in prayer. To *paraphrase* is to clarify by expansion and the poet knows prayer to be the elucidation and growth of his soul. It is his *heart in pilgrimage*. A *plummet* measures the depth of water and *sounding* means fathoming, exploring the as yet unseen realities of *heav'n and earth*. Herbert then uses another instrument as an image but, this time, one of warfare, an *engine* that besieges God and so suggests that prayer has its combative side as God tries to use it to save us from ourselves, whereas we can use it simply to enforce our own prejudices. It can make for some discomfort. The *sinners towre* may refer to a city's watchtower that looks out for its citizens, making it a place of safe refuge, but it also recalls the tower of Babel, an edifice constructed from pride and presumption. It is up to us which tower we make prayer into.

Prayer (I)

In many religious myths, the gods show their anger in thunder and lightning, but Herbert calls prayer *reversed thunder* – the rage is returned, as it were, and peace is offered. The *spear* that lanced Jesus' side on the cross is used to describe prayer because, through its inflicted hurt, it nevertheless helped grace to pour out on the world. Herbert then refers to our busy, distracted working lives as *the six-daies world* that, in an hour of prayer or worship, is *transposed*, rewritten, expressed in a different key so as to be understood too as a *kinde of tune*. He lays out those things that prayer brings to the soul by reflecting God, the one who loves us. These include *softnesse* – a mixture of suppleness and gentleness that every relationship needs.

The manna given by God as a gift to hungry people in a wilderness is in this poem *exalted*, lifted up in gratitude, as prayer keeps its daily promise to say thank you in *gladnesse of the best* and to see everywhere as having potential for communion. Prayer sees *heaven in ordinarie*, a sacrament of the present moment, and by praying we become *well drest*, the better version of ourselves and prepared for celebration. By bringing in *the milkie way*, the poet reminds us of the vast and beautiful mysteries that lie well beyond our comprehension and were once thought to be a roadway to heaven's palace. A *bird of Paradise*, or Huma bird, was believed to feed on dew there but, more importantly, was also thought never to perch on the earth, spending its entire life flying invisibly high, never at rest.

The final couplet gives four last glimpses into the nature of prayer with a change of tone. In the first, we ask whether he means *bels* on earth being heard in heaven or heavenly bells being heard on earth – or both. As *bloud* circulates around the body, giving life and energy, so prayer functions in the human soul. Then there is a mention of *the land of spices*. It recalls

Eden as well as the homeland of Jesus' ministry. It suggests beauty and welcome beyond the horizon. It is a sensual image as we imagine breathing in to enjoy the spice's aromas. Prayer enables us to appreciate and enjoy those things that bring zest to existence. Prayer creates a better-flavoured, more savoury world.

The last two words of the poem strike the heart: *something understood*. Prayer helps us, perhaps, to understand something about the ultimate trustworthiness of reality. Alternatively, prayer is something that always 'stands under', aware that God is the source of our wonder. If anything is clear about this poem – and, indeed, about all Herbert's poems – it is that he believed very deeply, without love nothing can be understood. Prayer is the place where we and God come to understand each other a little better.

The Holy Scriptures (I)

Oh Book! infinite sweetnesse! let my heart
    Suck ev'ry letter, and a hony gain,
    Precious for any grief in any part;
To cleare the breast, to mollifie all pain.

Thou art all health, health thriving, till it make
    A full eternitie: thou art a masse
    Of strange delights, where we may wish & take.
Ladies, look here; this is the thankfull glasse,

That mends the lookers eyes: this is the well
    That washes what it shows. Who can indeare
    Thy praise too much? thou art heav'ns Lidger here,
Working against the states of death and hell.

    Thou art joyes handsell: heav'n lies flat in thee,
    Subject to ev'ry mounters bended knee.

This poem begins by addressing what Herbert in another place
calls 'the book of books, the storehouse and magazine of life
and comfort', the Bible (1991, p. 204). He calls it The Holy
Scriptures and devotes two poems to it, this being the first
of them. With a post-Reformation zeal for the word, Herbert
writes what, in effect, is a love sonnet, passionate and intense,

in praise of the words he believes God has written to human-kind, with a similarly ardent and expressive love.

The Bible is *infinite sweetnesse* for Herbert. He wants his heart to *suck ev'ry letter* like a bee that makes honey to be enjoyed as both delicious and medicinal. Like the psalmist who prays, 'how sweet are thy words unto my throat: yea, sweeter than honey unto my mouth' (Psalm 119.103, BCP), Herbert wants to draw out the nutrients from the Scriptures. He continues by noting that the Bible is *precious* when we are grieving, when our feelings need to be put in order and we need solace for our internal anxieties.

The second stanza reveals that the Scriptures are full of health-giving properties, making the good in us thrive and building us up to the fullness and richness of eternity rather than simmering us down to the restricted vision of the world. It is a *masse/Of strange delights*, bewildering and inspiring in equal measure as it questions all our answers. The Bible creates a longing for God in us and reassures this yearning by showing us God's deeper longing for us. Addressing women of his day, Herbert says the Bible is the mirror that *mends the lookers eyes* by seeing ourselves as we really are, imperfect and redeemed. It is a *well* that cleans the reflection in its water as we look down. Herbert, it appears, could go on but stops by saying that nobody could do justice in praising the beauty and wisdom of the Scriptures.

He tries again, though. This time he refers to it as *heav'ns Lidger* – that is, resident ambassador – although it also sounds like 'ledger', which is a record book for keeping accounts. The Bible is God's ambassador *working against the states of death and hell*, the states of course being inside us, states of affairs and emotional states. The last couplet celebrates the Scriptures as *joyes handsell* or first instalment. *Heav'n lies flat* in the pages, but only those who approach those pages in prayer, on *bended knee*, will glimpse it. This last point is crucial. The Bible is abused if used as a tool for self-justification, as ammunition in argument or as a back-up to preconceived prejudices. A text taken out of context is usually a pretext for something. We must approach the Scriptures with humility, always aware of our need and not our clever understanding. For the Christian, such humility is never thinking less of ourselves but, rather, thinking of ourselves less.

Herbert is clear: the Bible is a *precious* resource for the praying and open soul longing to love God more and be drawn in deeper by God's love for his creation. It is the book that helps us to conform to Christ by making us willing to rethink. As we have discovered before, Herbert was a reader of St Augustine and it was he who wrote a helpful reminder to those who praise the Bible (*On Christian Doctrine*, I, 36, 40):

> Whosoever, then, thinks that he understands the Holy Scriptures, or any part of them, but puts such an interpretation upon them as does not tend to build up this twofold love of God and our neighbour, does not yet understand them as he ought.

I have no doubt at all that Herbert would have said a very loud 'Amen'.

Even-song

Blest be the God of love,
Who gave me eyes, and light, and power this day,
Both to be busie, and to play.
But much more blest be God above,

Who gave me sight alone,
Which to himself he did denie:
For when he sees my waies, I dy:
But I have got his sonne, and he hath none.

What have I brought thee home
For this thy love? have I discharg'd the debt,
Which this dayes favour did beget?
I ranne; but all I brought, was fome.

Thy diet, care, and cost
Do end in bubbles, balls of winde;
Of winde to thee whom I have crost,
But balls of wilde-fire to my troubled minde.

Yet still thou goest on,
And now with darknesse closest wearie eyes,
Saying to man, *It doth suffice*:
Henceforth repose; your work is done.

Even-song

Thus in thy Ebony box
Thou dost inclose us, till the day
Put our amendment in our way,
And give new wheels to our disorder'd clocks.

I muse, which shows more love,
The day or night: that is the gale, this th'harbour;
That is the walk, and this the arbour;
Or that the garden, this the grove.

My God, thou art all love.
Not one poore minute scapes thy breast,
But brings a favour from above;
And in this love, more then in bed, I rest.

Evensong is the service of confession and praise celebrated towards the end of the day. It is the service that has the two canticles of the Magnificat and the Nunc Dimittis within it. They are spoken by young and old, man and woman, one near to a birth and one near to a death, capturing human life and the way God is weaved within it. Both speakers of the canticles, Mary and Simeon, know that God's heart pours out on his world, especially on those the world laughs at or ignores. The two canticles of Evensong are the two compasses that point us towards the peaceful harbour of the human soul, but also to the humility, courage and generosity with which we must make the journey there.

This poem is Herbert's poetic equivalent and begins, as all prayers try to do, with gratitude. He blesses God for being a God of love who has given him *eyes, and light, and power this day*, allowing him to work and *play*. But even more, Herbert

31

is thankful to God for turning a blind eye to his *waies* and therefore saving him. Herbert has got God's *sonne* on his side through the incarnation, whereby God willingly gave him up and handed him over to the world, and still God refuses to look at the sins of human beings, such is his love.

Herbert asks what he has done to thank God. Has he given back appropriately for the *favour* he has received? Well, he concludes, he *ranne* through the day, but all he seems to have generated is *fome*, froth, like an animal's perspiration. God's loving way, his *diet* of care and gifts, all seem to come to nothing in Herbert, he confesses. He is a man of *bubbles* and insubstantial hot air who God can see as the one who has *crost* him (a pun on having also put Christ on the cross) and that, when he thinks about it, badly troubles his own mind.

God carries on with Herbert as if none of this were the case. He appears to close his *wearie eyes* and says to him, and to all of us, *It doth suffice:/Henceforth repose; your work is done.* It is as if God were saying, like a loving parent to a child getting into bed, 'It's OK. I know there's been some bad behaviour and that you're worried, but get into bed now and sleep well. I love you.'

God closes us into his *Ebony box*, the night, until the day breaks and another chance is given to disordered lives, like a new mechanism in a clock. It was believed that ebony had medicinal qualities and was able to neutralize poisons. So, the night brings a healing peace. Herbert then asks which reveals God's love more, the day or the night? He then lists apparent opposites, so that, for example, one is the *gale,* in which all the stress and dangers of the day are played out, and the other is the *harbour,* a place of refuge and rest. His conclusion is not one or the other but both. God is *all love* and not a minute passes by during the day or night when God's heart of love isn't pouring out blessings.

The last line is a beautiful example of how Herbert so often reflects on the nature of God's love and, through it, comes to a self-acceptance and peaceful resolution within. It is also a line that evokes the intimate, watchful, protecting love of God who, as that loving parent mentioned earlier, hears our breathing as we sleep and feels proud and loving towards his own. *And in this love, more then in bed, I rest.*

The Windows

Lord, how can man preach thy eternall word?
      He is a brittle crazie glasse:
Yet in thy temple thou dost him afford
        This glorious and transcendent place,
        To be a window, through thy grace.

But when thou dost anneal in glasse thy storie,
      Making thy life to shine within
The holy Preachers; then the light and glorie
        More rev'rend grows, & more doth win:
        Which else shows watrish, bleak, & thin.

Doctrine and life, colours and lights, in one
      When they combine and mingle, bring
A strong regard and aw: but speech alone
        Doth vanish like a flaring thing,
        And in the eare, not conscience ring.

George Herbert's friend and fellow poet John Donne once wrote: 'It is not the depth, nor the wit, nor the eloquence of the Preacher that pierces us, but his nearnesse' (1953–1962, III, 5). People are affected by a preacher whose humanity seems near to their own. A shared sense of human experience is the heart of the resonance that the preacher seeks to create in order to communicate words that might help to reimagine the world.

In this poem, Herbert pursues the idea that it is not just the preacher's words, however, that matter. There must be some integration, even if it is unresolved or in a lived tension, between the life and behaviour of the preacher and his or her message from the pulpit. All preachers know the inevitability of being a hypocrite as they try to steer a course in human hearts, not least their own, towards the kingdom of God, even as they live within the conflicted world of today. As one preacher said to me, 'I want to try and help people to have that relationship with God that I only wish I had myself.'

No wonder, then, that Herbert begins with the question *Lord, how can man preach thy eternall word?* He understands that human beings are *brittle* and *crazie* – that is, full of cracks and imperfections – and refers to them being fractured *glasse*. It brings to mind St Paul's reflection that 'now we see through a glass, darkly' (1 Corinthians 13.12). God, like an economical cook who opens the fridge and just uses what's there, takes the imperfect glass and uses it as a window. The preacher can hardly believe that he or she merits this glorious and transcendent vocation. It could only ever be initiated through grace.

God seeks, continues Herbert, to *anneal*, burn colours, into the *glasse* by his *storie*, the gospel. The preacher's life then shines, like stained glass, with God's life, and genuine light is encountered as the *glorie* of God, not of the preacher, grows. If the preacher doesn't open himself or herself up to this graceful relationship, the result from the pulpit tends to be watered down – *watrish*, often bleak or thin. There will always be less to this preaching than meets the ear.

What brings *aw* and strong regard from the congregation is, says Herbert, when one's beliefs and one's life seem to translate each other. *Regard* can refer to observation. Preaching full of grace helps people to develop their attention and their ability to notice things. When *doctrine and life* both *combine and mingle*, they will, in the words of a prayer in the Book of Common Prayer, 'set forth thy true and lively Word'. The *colours* of the preacher's human experience, and the life being lived, are moulded with the richness of the gospel and form a window through which the sun can stream.

If, though, the preacher is focused only on the sound of his or her own rhetorical voice, the cleverness of the argument or the level of applause coming from the audience at the end, then no matter how hard the preacher has tried, the words will *vanish like a flaring thing*. The ear may have been tickled for a while, but there has been no resonance or dislocation in the conscience of the hearer. A sermon can attract and inform, but unless it moves, stirs the listener into a deeper longing for God, it cannot be distinguished from a lecture. Like a flower sitting in the sunlight streaming through the window, hearers should want to turn more towards the light in order to have their full dignity and beauty revealed.

Lancelot Andrewes, Herbert's mentor when he was a young man, told preachers in a sermon in Whitehall on Ash Wednesday, 1619, that it was their charge to preach to people 'not what for the present they would hear but what in another day they would wish they had heard'. Herbert agreed with his teacher with all his heart.

Content

Peace mutt'ring thoughts, and do not grudge to keep
      Within the walls of your own breast:
Who cannot on his own bed sweetly sleep,
      Can on anothers hardly rest.

Gad not abroad at ev'ry quest and call
      Of an untrained hope or passion.
To court each place or fortune that doth fall,
      Is wantonnesse in contemplation.

Mark how the fire in flints doth quiet lie,
      Content and warm t' it self alone:
But when it would appeare to others eye,
      Without a knock it never shone.

Give me the pliant minde, whose gentle measure
      Complies and suits with all estates;
Which can let loose to a crown, and yet with pleasure
      Take up within a cloisters gates.

This soul doth span the world, and hang content
      From either pole unto the centre:
Where in each room of the well-furnisht tent
      He lies warm, and without adventure.

Content

The brags of life are but a nine dayes wonder;
        And after death the fumes that spring
From private bodies make as big a thunder,
        As those which rise from a huge King.

Onely thy Chronicle is lost; and yet
        Better by worms be all once spent,
Then to have hellish moths still gnaw and fret
        Thy name in books, which may not rent:

When all thy deeds, whose brunt thou feel'st alone,
        Are chaw'd by others pens and tongue;
And as their wit is, their digestion,
        Thy nourisht fame is weak or strong.

Then cease discoursing soul, till thine own ground,
        Do not thy self or friends importune.
He that by seeking hath himself once found,
        Hath euer found a happie fortune.

W. H. Auden believed of Herbert that 'one does not get the impression from his work that the temptations of the flesh were a spiritual menace to him ... His struggle was with worldliness, the desire to move in high circles, to enjoy fame and power' (1973, p. 8). This poem has been called a 'sermon to himself' by Herbert (Benet, 1984, p. 136) as he looks at this ambition face on and confesses the desire to change.

    The title of the poem, 'Content', plays on the words 'contentment' and 'content' – needing the first and knowing that what lies in him, the contents of his soul, will either lead him to find it or lose it. It begins with Herbert asking his *mutt'ring thoughts* to calm down and stay within him, not be tempted to look elsewhere. 'A Christian's eyes ought to be turned inward,' wrote Thomas Fuller in 1640, 'yet how many are there whose home is to be always abroad' (p. 69). Herbert doesn't want any undisciplined longings to lead him into an internal state that he doesn't want to be in. Just assessing how to get every high or influential position going at court or elsewhere is *wantonnesse in contemplation* – a sinful thought.

The third stanza reflects how one doesn't see the fire that rests unseen in a flint until someone strikes it. In the same way, it is right that your potential is not forced or cunningly propelled on to the world. One should contentedly wait for the *knock* on your door that invites you into the public eye. Anyway, he continues, he wants a *pliant minde*, flexible and gentle, that can relate to people of all types and backgrounds. He wants a mind like that of King Charles V of Spain, who abdicated in 1556 to enter a monastery. Such spiritual strength, upturning the world's values, lies in the mind that can *let loose to a crown, and yet with pleasure/Take up within a cloisters gates*.

To have such a mind as this, explores the fifth verse, means that, wherever you find yourself in this world, and wherever you temporarily reside in this mortal life, you will lie *warm* and without needing to spend energy on adventurously climbing and competing up ladders. The *brags of life*, writes Herbert, are gone before you know it and death strikes us all down. The gases that are rumoured to have made Henry VIII's corpse explode and William the Conqueror's to emit foul-smelling fumes is proof that, in death, we are all the same. Crowns tarnish very quickly. It's preferable to be eaten up by worms than to have your name in history books where *hellish moths* will *gnaw and fret* at your name and disputed reputation. The penultimate stanza concludes that only we know who we are and what we did in this life. Others wade in with their wit, *pens and tongue* after we are gone and our afterlife, as it were, is in their hands – they make our fame weak or strong.

The insight that Herbert gains from all this is found in the last stanza. He tells his soul to stop scheming, anxiously going from one thought to another, but simply to *till thine own ground*, tend to your own humus (the root of 'humility'). He tells his soul to stop bothering himself or friends, presumably trying to feather his nest a bit more and be noticed. The last two lines summarize the way to contentment. It is to review what your own content is and whether it makes you truly content. If you can find yourself, in such a distracted world, and be at home there, then you have really found a *happie fortune*.

If this poem is Herbert's 'sermon to himself', then the text for the sermon seems clear: 'For what shall it profit a man, if he shall gain the whole world, and lose his own soul?' (Mark 8.36). The mythologist Joseph Campbell noted that human beings usually spend the first half of their life trying to climb up on to the roof, only to discover when they are there that it is the wrong house. This 'midlife crisis' is when we can choose to re-evaluate our life, asking what principles and values we want the rest of our life to be built on. For Herbert, such scrutiny and transformation were part of a serious soul's journey in a life divinely made for joy, for contentment.

The Quidditie

My God, a verse is not a crown,
No point of honour, or gay suit,
No hawk, or banquet, or renown,
Nor a good sword, nor yet a lute:

It cannot vault, or dance, or play;
It never was in *France* or *Spain*;
Nor can it entertain the day
With a great stable or domain:

It is no office, art, or news,
Nor the Exchange, or busie Hall;
But it is that which while I use
I am with thee, and *Most take all*.

What on earth is a quidditie? Well, it can either refer to the essence of something, that which answers the question *Quid est?* – 'What is it?' – or it can mean a quibble, usually over something pedantic or oversubtle. We find, as we so often do with Herbert's titles, that both meanings come into play in the poem. We discover here the world quibbling over its values and social ladders and, at the same time, it is a poem in search of something more profound and worthy of a life's pursuit. It is very much a poem for an age that is more comfortable with what it has than with what it is ultimately for.

In Herbert's sonnet 'Prayer (I)', he builds up an understanding of what prayer might be by a layering of images, one after another, that don't naturally relate but which, brought together, build a collage whose beauty makes you want to try it out and pray. In some early publications 'The Quidditie' also had the title 'Prayer', but instead of a list of positive nouns and verbs, Herbert accumulates what has been called 'flaunting negatives' (Stein, 1968, p. 19) as to what poetry is not. It is not a *crown*, because it has no earthly power or sovereignty. It doesn't threaten or boost one's honour, nor is it a *gay suit*, something happily and ambitiously chased.

Herbert continues by taking us into the lives of the aristocrats and courtiers. Poetry isn't a sport, like hunting with hawks, or an elaborate meal with a lot of wasted food, nor is it the game of fame that makes us all so obsessive. It is not *a good sword, not yet a lute*, neither a defence nor a diversion; it can't ride a horse, perform in dance and drama nor think itself stylish because it imitates the dress and etiquette of fashionable countries. Poetry can't bring people back to a large family estate and entertain.

After the courtly world, we are taken into that of business. Poetry isn't an *office* or a position. It isn't a cunning art, nor is it gossip. It is not the *Exchange*, a place for consumerism and commercialism, nor a loud *Hall*, where business transactions are done and money is the monarch.

After all this one expects to be told what poetry is, not just what it isn't. Instead, Herbert refrains and simply says that it is *that which, while I use/I am with thee*. As he uses poetry, reads it, writes and revises it, prays it and gives deep attention to it, so it becomes a place of sacred encounter. He knows that he is with God when with poetry. The distillation, the freshness and surprise of poetry, its invitation into the deeper currents, all make it holy ground. Poetry explores the immense intimacies and the intimate immensities of life and the world, and it is in these that God's presence burns like a scorching and defrosting fire.

What do we make of the last three words? It is a version of 'winner takes all' in card games, where you trust in the game by surrendering your cards and money. In the poem, Herbert decides to renounce his interest in the ways of the world and to be a poet who sits with God as he works. By doing this he 'wins', but so does God. God, who may be described as *Most*, also takes all of Herbert to himself for safekeeping. The last word is *all*, a word sometimes used by Herbert for God. In his poem 'The Invitation', he writes: 'Where is all, there all should be.' The last word of a poem that has ploughed through a whole list of words which are not about *all* and everyone, but about how we can rise above them all, must be *God*.

I find this poem moving as I too believe myself to be with God when encountering poetry. 'If I knew where poems came from,' said Michael Longley in an interview with Kate Kellaway many years ago, 'I'd go there.' Herbert has started the journey.

Deniall

When my devotions could not pierce
                Thy silent eares;
Then was my heart broken, as was my verse:
    My breast was full of fears
                And disorder:

My bent thoughts, like a brittle bow,
                Did flie asunder:
Each took his way; some would to pleasures go,
    Some to the warres and thunder
                Of alarms.

As good go any where, they say,
                As to benumme
Both knees and heart, in crying night and day,
    Come, come, my God, O come,
                But no hearing.

O that thou shouldst give dust a tongue
                To crie to thee,
And then not heare it crying! all day long
    My heart was in my knee,
                But no hearing.

Therefore my soul lay out of sight,
Untun'd, unstrung:
My feeble spirit, unable to look right,
Like a nipt blossome, hung
Discontented.

O cheer and tune my heartlesse breast,
Deferre no time;
That so thy favours granting my request,
They and my minde may chime,
And mend my ryme.

This poem is a good example of the honesty that readers quickly come to appreciate in Herbert's work. The title is 'Deniall' and we instantly understand as we read that Herbert must be referring to God apparently refusing his prayerful requests and the heartache that comes from this. The other denial may, however, be Herbert's, in refusing to trust God's care and love of him. In rhetoric, denial is a contradiction and here it is in this poem: both God and Herbert are apparently denying each other, although expressing this with frankness and openness means that they are in a healthy relationship at the same time.

The poem takes the form of a prayer and begins with Herbert referring to his own devotions and to God's *silent eares*. We wonder if this God is capricious or indifferent, and we feel for the poet as both his heart and his writing become broken. Herbert becomes *full of fears/And disorder*. The form of the poem, disjointed as it is, embodies on the page this spiritual disorder of Herbert's inner landscape.

His thoughts fly about without any direction or purpose, like an arrow from a broken *bow*. He finds himself pursuing pleasures one day and *warres* the next. *Alarms* are calls to battle. He has no centre in his soul any more and so finds distractions and ways of proving himself that ultimately let him down and prove nothing except that he is vulnerable. He prays endlessly for God to come and bring some reassurance and hope, but there is *no hearing*, it seems.

Herbert, frustrated, thinks it strange that God should give human beings a tongue with which to speak to him and then not listen to them. His heart is completely in his prayer as he kneels, but this doesn't appear to mean anything to God because there is still *no hearing*. The repetition of this lets fall an ominous shadow of doubt and dereliction.

So, continues Herbert, the consequence of this is that his soul became like an abandoned musical instrument – *untun'd, unstrung*. His spirits are low, he can't make sense of things and, like a spring bud iced by a sudden frost, he hangs dejected with all sense of potential and purpose taken from him. Yet, still Herbert prays and the last stanza calls on God to cheer and tune his *heartlesse breast* and to do it immediately, without delay. He asks that what is given to him by God, and the mind which receives it, may *chime* so that Herbert's *ryme* both as poet and as Christian may be mended. What we notice is that the last two lines of the poem do rhyme, whereas the last two lines of the other stanzas do not, and this means that, as Herbert prays, so his prayer is being answered. The rhyme is restored as it is sought. 'You would not seek Me if you had not already found Me' is how the philosopher Pascal voices this paradox of the soul in his *Pensées* (Section 7, 553).

The silence of God is necessary for Christians. It reminds us that what we long for most, ultimately, must elude us, for a God who can be easily understood is not a God worth worshipping. God gives us enough to look, but never quite enough to fully find. As a defence against our idolatry, he often becomes silent so that our certainties are dismantled back into faith and we learn to speak the foreign language of God again. The philosopher Martin Buber reminds us that a divine eclipse does not mean God is dead (1957). It might mean he has never been nearer.

Vanitie (I)

The fleet Astronomer can bore,
And thred the spheres with his quick-piercing minde:
He views their stations, walks from doore to doore,
Surveys, as if he had design'd
To make a purchase there: he sees their dances,
And knoweth long before,
Both their full-ey'd aspects, and secret glances.

The nimble Diver with his side
Cuts through the working waves, that he may fetch
His dearely-earned pearl, which God did hide
On purpose from the ventrous wretch;
That he might save his life, and also hers,
Who with excessive pride
Her own destruction and his danger wears.

The subtil Chymick can devest
And strip the creature naked, till he finde
The callow principles within their nest:
There he imparts to them his minde,
Admitted to their bed-chamber, before
They appear trim and drest
To ordinarie suitours at the doore.

Vanitie (I)

What hath not man sought out and found,
But his deare God? who yet his glorious law
Embosomes in us, mellowing the ground
        With showres and frosts, with love & aw,
So that we need not say, Where's this command?
        Poore man, thou searchest round
To finde out *death*, but missest *life* at hand.

The world of experimental science was flourishing dur-
ing Herbert's lifetime but, like many before him, such as
St Augustine, he was concerned that the relentless efforts to
know the facts of creation might somehow replace the desire
to know the Creator himself. This poem, 'Vanitie (I)', gives
voice to that concern. Human knowledge is a vanity project,
he believes, if divorced from the knowledge of God. He says in
another poem called 'Mattens' that 'Man did not heav'n and
earth create,/Yet studies them, not him by whom they be.'

Herbert begins by thinking of astronomers. They trace the
spheres with *quick-piercing minde* but, rather like someone
looking to pick up a prostitute, they walk from *doore to doore*
and survey as if to make a purchase. They know the dances of
the stars, their positions and *secret glances*, brief and sudden
movements. It's hard not to conclude that Herbert is here sug-
gesting, in the words of one critic, 'stargazing is prurient in its
own way' (Skulsky, 1987, p. 90).

He then considers the diver (maybe a pun on Dives in the
Gospel, who ignored the poor man at his gate) who swims
through the *working waves*, the agitated sea, in order to get
the pearl that God has hidden away from the adventurous
explorer. God has hidden it so that the man doesn't have to

risk his life and the excessive pride of the woman wearing it won't be her moral destruction.

Then Herbert turns to the chemist, which may also refer to the alchemist, who undresses the material creation to find the naked, fundamental elements of the world. The chemist takes these into the inner recesses of his or her mind and works out how to make them well *drest/To ordinarie suitours.*

The last stanza brings the reflection to a conclusion. What hasn't humanity discovered, except *deare God*? This God intimately places his law, conscience and the sense of reality that is worthy of trust into our hearts. God mellows *the ground* with the seasons of the year and the seasons of the heart so we don't need to go looking. It is all there before us and in us. A human being is *poore*, thinks Herbert, if he searches endlessly for facts. Like the ex-priest who becomes a seller of encyclopedias in John Updike's novel *The Beauty of the Lilies*, he has every fact literally to hand, but is still left alone and bewildered, not knowing anything. Information alone does not help the soul's formation and cannot replace wisdom. We miss *life at hand* if we think it does.

Whether Herbert can be justly condemned as some sort of anti-intellectual in this poem is unlikely, to my mind. I think, instead, he simply wishes to make the search for the truths of the world and the truth of God simultaneous and mutually enriching. St Augustine (Bourke, 1974, p. 123) again, in one of his sermons, probably influenced his thinking:

Some people, in order to discover God, read a book. But there is a great book: the very appearance of created things. Look above and below, note, read. God whom you want to discover, did not make the letters with ink; he put in front of your eyes the very things that he made. Can you ask for a louder voice than that?

Vertue

Sweet day, so cool, so calm, so bright,
The bridall of the earth and skie:
The dew shall weep thy fall to night;
     For thou must die.

Sweet rose, whose hue angrie and brave
Bids the rash gazer wipe his eye:
Thy root is ever in its grave,
     And thou must die.

Sweet spring, full of sweet days and roses,
A box where sweets compacted lie;
My musick shows ye have your closes,
     And all must die.

Onely a sweet and virtuous soul,
Like season'd timber, never gives;
But though the whole world turn to coal,
     Then chiefly lives.

There is a tradition in some poetry of reminding the reader that life is short and everything comes to an end and, therefore, you should seize the day and enjoy life to the full before it is taken from you. To begin with, one might think that this is the nature of Herbert's 'Vertue'. In a somewhat melancholic tone, but with lyrical tenderness and simplicity, the poem points us to the transitory nature of all that is. The surprise lies in Herbert's conclusion. His is not an urgent or indulgent call to live in the present but, in fact, the opposite. He beckons us to live in tune with what is not passing but eternal, the things that transcend the noise and intensities of the 'now'.

The word *sweet* is used five times in the poem. It can refer to pleasant sensory qualities and it can refer to something that is dear or precious to us. The first verse awakens us to a *sweet day, cool, calm* and *bright.* Herbert sees the earth he stands on and the sky gloriously above in a marriage, a *bridall,* a day to celebrate and be joyful in. He knows that the day will end, though, and, like tears, the wet *dew* will voice the world's bereavement as night falls and the day dies. His use of the word *fall* inevitably invokes the wider sense of our fractured and fragile human life, alienated from ourselves and from our God. As Philip Larkin asks in his poem, 'Where can we live but days?' (2012, p. 60).

We are then presented with a rose – its *hue angrie and brave,* referring to its red flush of colour and its strikingly beautiful form. To understand the plight of the flower – its inevitable fading, drooping and death – brings anyone who has time to stop and look cause to *wipe his eye.* From Roman days, the rose has been thought to have medicinal properties to heal eyes, but here it is the cause of smarting tears as we look at the rose and think too, probably, of ourselves and those we love. Our *root too is ever in its grave.* The words addressed to us on Ash Wednesday won't let us forget it: 'you are dust, and to dust you shall return' (Genesis 3.19, NRSV). A cross is made on our head, the hard case that holds the place where we make our decisions, and as it is marked, so it becomes the new compass for our will, priorities and values.

Then Herbert notes that even the first season of the year – the season of birth and bulbs, of blossom and nests – is also mortal. Spring, he says, is a *box where sweets compacted lie*, a place where herbal and floral perfumes are stored or, maybe if it is a music box, where the music and energies of life are to be found. In his poem 'Church-Musick', Herbert refers to music as being the 'sweetest of sweets' and this too teaches him about closes and life's cadences.

The last stanza has a different feel. We move from the riotous colours of spring to *season'd timber*, matured and hardened. Virtue, the very opposite of vice, is that which outshines and outlives a bright day, a lovely flower and the beauty of spring. Like wood that has been tested for purpose, the *virtuous soul never gives*, it doesn't warp under pressure or over time. Again, one might sense that the wood of the cross is a resonance that shouldn't be ignored here – the wood that held the one truly sweet and virtuous soul. Herbert ends his poem with the image of the earth ending in fire, not an un-realistic picture as climate change remains relatively ignored by influential world leaders. Even though our world will *turn to coal*, nevertheless, the loving soul will not disappear but will live more fully through the life of the one who once lay on timber but is now our chief cornerstone and *chiefly lives*.

'Vertue' is a poem that reminds us sorrow is written into the contract of life and, though we assemble a life of loves, we pay the cost of them in grief and loss. This might be the end of our philosophy and lead us to some radical, maybe destructive, decisions as to how to live this life through. Herbert is no *rash gazer*. He comprehends by a study on our losses that without love, nothing can be understood. If we learn to use things and love people, not the other way around, we discover an eternal truth about truths that are eternal – a thought also expressed much later by Desmond Tutu in *An African Prayer Book* (2006):

> Goodness is stronger than evil;
> Love is stronger than hate;
> Light is stronger than darkness;
> Life is stronger than death;
> Victory is ours through Him who loves us.

The Pearl. Matth. 13

I know the wayes of learning; both the head
And pipes that feed the presse, and make it runne;
What reason hath from nature borrowed,
Or of it self, like a good huswife, spunne
In laws and policie; what the starres conspire,
What willing nature speaks, what forc'd by fire;
Both th' old discoveries, and the new-found seas,
The stock and surplus, cause and historie;
All these stand open, or I have the keyes:
                    Yet I love thee.

I know the wayes of honour; what maintains
The quick returns of courtesie and wit:
In vies of favours whether partie gains,
When glorie swells the heart, and moldeth it
To all expressions both of hand and eye,
Which on the world a true-love-knot may tie,
And bear the bundle, wheresoe're it goes:
How many drammes of spirit there must be
To sell my life unto my friends or foes:
                    Yet I love thee.

I know the wayes of pleasure, the sweet strains,
The lullings and the relishes of it;
The propositions of hot bloud and brains;

What mirth and musick mean; what love and wit
Have done these twentie hundred years, and more:
I know the projects of unbridled store:
My stuffe is flesh, not brasse; my senses live,
And grumble oft, that they have more in me
Then he that curbs them, being but one to five:
                    Yet I love thee.

I know all these, and have them in my hand.
Therefore not sealed, but with open eyes
I flie to thee, and fully understand
Both the main sale, and the commodities;
And at what rate and price I have thy love;
With all the circumstances that may move:
Yet through the labyrinths, not my groveling wit,
But thy silk twist let down from heav'n to me,
Did both conduct and teach me, how by it
                    To climb to thee.

Only five of Herbert's poems have a biblical reference in the title and this is one of them. It points us to Jesus' teaching in Matthew's Gospel (13.45–46): 'Again, the kingdom of heaven is like unto a merchant man, seeking goodly pearls: who, when he had found a pearl of great price, went and sold all that he had, and bought it.'

A poem with a complex rhyme scheme, it has four verses, each with nine long lines and a last short line that startles.

Herbert was, in many ways, a man of the world. In this poem, he admits it. He knows what the world has to offer because, in his own life, he had been privileged enough to enjoy much of it. This, however, is a poem of renunciation and conversion. The key word that repeats three times is *yet*. Herbert is aware and has experienced the pleasures of life, yet he also knows more and needs more. He knows that the things we pursue and build our reputations with are nothing compared to the love of God and its riches for human living. He knows that a human self will be more itself when it is not so selfish. He has discovered that restless hearts find their true rest only in their Creator.

The poem begins by referring to a world Herbert knew a lot about – that of education. His university career had shown him the *wayes of learning*. Using a metaphor from pressing oil and from a printing press, he tells of how the brain will *runne* in pursuit of logic, law and astronomy. Some knowledge comes from observation of nature and some has to be *forc'd by fire*, like heat is used in a chemical experiment. We can learn old wisdom and add to it ourselves, *stock and surplus*, and it can be immediately accessible or researched over time as if with a slow-turning key. There is fulfilment to be had in such learning and, though the temptation of intellect is arrogance and intellectual pride, to learn is a wonderful pursuit in life. Yet, says Herbert, we are made for more. Where do you think the stress should be in line 10? On *yet* or *I* or *thee*?

Herbert also knew about court life and the *wayes of honour*, the need for quick wit and competing for favours, the way human *glorie swells the heart* and enters a love match with the world that can quickly turn into being servile to its many demands to be successful. It's like pouring out your soul in small measures, *drammes*, like whisky, to please friends or get one up on an enemy. We can end up in this life with a lot to live with but little to live for. The way of the world is exhaustingly gladiatorial and precarious.

The third verse becomes rather musical in its talk of *pleasure* and this is understandable as Herbert was a fine musician. Some of the phrasing has possible sexual overtones too. Herbert says that he understands the significance of *mirth and musick*, love and wit. He admits that he's a human being in need of all these things, not a *brasse* object. His five senses outnumber his reason and help him to relish life even when his head tells him to curb them.

Finally, Herbert says that, unlike falcons, which have their eyes sewn up to make them blind, he flies to heaven fully aware of the often pleasurable ways of this world that still hold in them all a sense of let-down. He knows the material advantages to be gained and the price of living according to the rules of the powerful. He also knows the cost of God's love, the sacrifice of Christ that pours out love on him. Herbert understands that his intellect or *groveling wit* (*groveling* literally meaning 'low or on one's belly', like the snake in Eden) is not the way to navigate life's labyrinths, as Theseus had to in the classical myth. Instead, like Ariadne's thread that guided him out of the maze, God has let down a *silk twist* to save him. This is a rope that helps pull us up towards God, out of the world's webs and warrens. Whether this silk twist is Christ or the Scriptures or the life of prayer or something else, we can't be sure. John Calvin wrote that the knowledge of God 'is for us like an inexplicable labyrinth unless we are conducted into it by the thread of the Word' (Veith, 1985, p. 195). What is clear is that it is God who has stepped in to raise and so liberate Herbert.

Part of us is always very at home in the world, but is it our better part? Sin can often be the addiction to being less than ourselves. The sharp surprise of the last lines of each verse interrogates our own values, capitulations and levels of spiritual seriousness. This poem always reminds me of St Augustine's prayer in his *Confessions*, that God would grant him to know himself so that he could then know God.

Unkindnesse

Lord, make me coy and tender to offend:
In friendship, first I think, if that agree,
        Which I intend,
    Unto my friends intent and end.
I would not use a friend, as I use Thee.

If any touch my friend, or his good name;
It is my honour and my love to free
        His blasted fame
    From the least spot or thought of blame.
I could not use a friend, as I use Thee.

My friend may spit upon my curious floore:
Would he have gold? I lend it instantly;
        But let the poore,
    And thou within them starve at doore.
I cannot use a friend, as I use Thee.

When that my friend pretendeth to a place,
I quit my interest, and leave it free:
        But when thy grace
    Sues for my heart, I thee displace,
Nor would I use a friend, as I use Thee.

Yet can a friend what thou hast done fulfill?
O write in brasse, *My God upon a tree*
His bloud did spill
Onely to purchase my good-will:
Yet use I not my foes, as I use Thee.

I said in the Introduction that I believe Herbert had an over-whelming and consistent understanding of God as his friend. In this poem, he reflects on how he treats his friends and then compares this to how he treats God. He is unnerved by his findings and makes confession.

He first asks that he may be *coy*, reserved and *tender*, reluctant to cause offence. He says that, when it comes to friends, he always asks whether what he is about to do, or is doing, fits in with his friends' interests and welfare. Because he doesn't ask the same question of his God, he painfully admits *I would not use a friend, as I use Thee.*

If anyone puts one of his friends down and darkens his reputation, Herbert says, he does all he can to put it right and to stand up for him, *from the least spot or thought of blame.* He does not do the same for God when God is blasphemed or ridiculed. He would let his friend *spit* on his *curious*, beautifully made floor and if his friend needed money, he would give it to him. But knowing that what we do for the least, we do for God, when he ignores the needs of the *poore*, he is ignoring his God and not treating him as a friend. Likewise, he continues, when a friend has an aspiration and hope for a place in life, he sacrifices his own interests and tries to help, but when God's grace wants to make a home in his heart, he turns him out.

The last stanza turns the table and asks if God has been a friend to him. What he concludes he wants written *in brasse,* permanently inscribed for all to see, not least to remind Herbert himself. God sacrificed himself, gave his life, to show his love as a friend and assure him of his *good-will*. Herbert's last line hits home: he wouldn't treat his enemies as he treats God and yet God has given him everything he has, even stepping in to save him from himself by losing his own life, for his friend, and still Herbert treats him worse than any foe.

We all have our thoughts about friends, and I don't mean the thousands of friends people take pride in on social media but the one or two who have changed our lives for good, maybe at some cost to us both. There is mutual freedom in friendship and a bravery to speak honestly, a resistance to put each other or ourselves on pedestals. Friendship can help to remove masks that eat into our faces and enable a willingness to hear things about ourselves which we can hardly bear to hear, but know will help us to grow if we do. Friends teach us not to skate over our thin ice so quickly, scared we may disappear through our cracks, but reach out to help, support and form the connection we crave in life. It was such a friend that God became to Herbert. His treatment of his friend shocked him when he thought about it. Giving a little thought to our own behaviour, we might see, once again, how Herbert proves a friend to us across the centuries.

Decay

Sweet were the dayes, when thou didst lodge with Lot,
Struggle with Jacob, sit with Gideon,
Advise with Abraham, when thy power could not
Encounter Moses strong complaints and mone:
   Thy words were then, *Let me alone.*

One might have sought and found thee presently
At some fair oak, or bush, or cave, or well:
Is my God this way? No, they would reply:
He is to Sinai gone, as we heard tell:
   List, ye may heare great Aarons bell.

But now thou dost thy self immure and close
In some one corner of a feeble heart:
Where yet both Sinne and Satan, thy old foes,
Do pinch and straiten thee, and use much art
   To gain thy thirds and little part.

I see the world grows old, when as the heat
Of thy great love once spread, as in an urn
Doth closet up it self, and still retreat,
Cold sinne still forcing it, till it return,
   And calling Justice, all things burn.

Human beings tend to look back and see past times as a golden age – so much so that those who actually used to live in that golden age also say things were more yellow than golden and not as good as previous years. In this poem, Herbert speaks to God and looks back to the age when God was intimately familiar with his people – lodging, struggling and sitting with, and advising, those such as Lot, Jacob, Gideon, Abraham and Moses. In fact, he says, God was so close to them that at one point he told Moses and his people to leave him alone because of their strong complaints and moaning.

Herbert reflects how, in those days, you could look and find God *presently*, immediately in the present, in ordinary day-to-day places like an *oak* tree, as Jacob did, or a *bush* (Moses), *cave* (Elijah) or *well* (Hagar). People would ask if God had gone *this way* and they would be told, as if he were a neighbour gone out for a stroll, that he had popped to Sinai. The reference to hearing the high priest *Aarons bell* recalls the bells of his robes, which would ring when he went into the holy place and stood before the Lord.

With all this in mind, Herbert rather laments the fact that now, in later times, such face-to-face familiarity isn't possible. Instead, God *immures* himself – that is, imprisons himself between walls – and props himself up in a corner of the human heart. He's not alone in there, though. His old foes *Sinne and Satan* restrict room, *pinch and straiten*, hem him in. These two enemies work hard to try and gain *thy thirds*, which was the property left to a widow on her husband's death, and take over the modest little part that God dwells in.

Herbert is watching the world grow old, decay, as the warmth of God's great love that once spread across the world in close and conversant ways is now, like ashes in an urn, locked up, and still in further retreat due to *cold sinne* doing its worst. One day, though, concludes Herbert, the love will return and reveal its heat again, on the last judgment day, and call *Justice* – and that will mean *all things burn*. One critic has said of this last line, 'In no other poem does Herbert invoke the last Judgment with such fury' (Bloch, 1985, p. 139). It's true that, on the whole, Herbert brings himself back to the love of God when thinking of God's justice. He does here, of course, but in terms of heat rather than light. The other thing worth noting in passing is that Herbert, throughout all his poems, hardly mentions hell. Love is the beginning and end of all things in Herbert's theology because God is the first and the last.

It is true that people of faith today know that faith must be an orientation towards the mystery rather than the domestication of God. Faith requires faith. Faith has more in common with trusting than with believing. Our worship of God begins in wonder and ends in humility, whereas in former days, when many thought God was 'theirs' and an enemy to their enemies, religion more often began with idolatry and ended in violence. That is why, for God to be just out of reach keeps us spiritually in check, stopping us getting above ourselves and maintaining a belief in a God who is not so at home in the world we have made as we like to imagine. Indeed, the phrase *hester panim*, the hiding of the face, occurs around forty times in the Hebrew Bible in reference to God. This poem, ultimately, gives voice, perhaps, to the restlessness of wanting to feel nearer to God but knowing that God is above, beside and within, now and every second.

Jordan (II)

When first my lines of heav'nly joyes made mention,
Such was their lustre, they did so excell,
That I sought out quaint words, and trim invention;
My thoughts began to burnish, sprout, and swell,
Curling with metaphors a plain intention,
Decking the sense, as if it were to sell.

Thousands of notions in my brain did runne,
Off'ring their service, if I were not sped:
I often blotted what I had begunne;
This was not quick enough, and that was dead.
Nothing could seem too rich to clothe the sunne,
Much lesse those joys which trample on his head.

As flames do work and winde, when they ascend,
So did I weave my self into the sense.
But while I bustled, I might heare a friend
Whisper, *How wide is all this long pretence!*
There is in love a sweetnesse readie penn'd:
Copie out onely that, and save expense.

The title of a poem is the first key we are given to open up the
rich and dense suggestions within the poem itself. Herbert gives
this poem the title 'Jordan', the name of the river mentioned
in 2 Kings 5, in which Elisha tells Naaman to wash seven times

so that he will be cleansed of his disease. It is also the river where John the Baptist baptized Jesus and where Jesus first heard words of love spoken to him from God (see, for example, Mark 1.11).

Herbert initiates us into the idea of cleansing and renewal – but of what? What does Herbert want to wash off? The immediate answer appears to be his elaborate and artificial playing with words that tries to strike the right literary pose and reveal what a good poet he is when, really, he should be trying to give simple voice to the nature and glory of God. In the first verse, he cleverly reveals how, as a poet, he can disguise self-regard as self-offering when he makes it ambiguous whether it is his lines or *heav'nly joyes* that so excelled. Perhaps he has forgotten the difference? He seeks out *quaint words* and *trim invention* – that is, he is trying to find ingenious and neat poetic sounds and formulas. As he gets going, it gets worse. His thoughts *burnish*, spread out and, *curling*, like a hairdresser, he takes what is plain and straight and complicates it in a vanity project. *Decking* means beautifying, as in 'decorating', and Herbert is aware of how he is guilty of an artistry that can be so excessive, it aims only to please the reader and not deepen the vision of God.

Herbert notes how his brain often goes to his head. He has, by the second verse, thousands of notions and if, through difficulty, he doesn't give up (*if I were not sped*), he will still frantically blot the page as he labours to find just the right words in the best order. Nothing seems too rich to *clothe the sunne*, he says, instantly revealing just how full of himself he can get. How can you clothe the sun? And how, even more, can you begin to congratulate yourself for a self-consciously styled language that believes it is honouring the other sun, the Son, and his crown of thorns? Herbert acknowledges how he can spiral in self-deceptions like some indiscriminating whirlwind fire.

Jordan (II)

While he *bustled* with all this exhausting imaginative activity, however, he heard a friend *whisper* and gently tell him how *wide* of the mark this artificial game is. Can't he see that *There is in love a sweetnesse readie penn'd*? As Jesus heard a loving voice at the Jordan, so does Herbert. In his poems he uses the word 'love' to refer to God, Christ and the Bible, and even the Christian life. Which does he mean here? Is this a reference to the Scriptures, and that if only he copies these out and *save expense*, he would have completed his proper vocation? Is divine love something you don't have to try hard to understand or please but simply let be, and so discover its quiet, unadorned fidelity? Or is this a reference to that other Word who lived among us and was penned in a prison and on a cross, the life we must imitate and who bears the cost of love?

Two final thoughts. It can be easy to miss the fact that it seems it is God who is being referred to as a friend. As we have seen, this is an image Herbert returns to and one we do well to take seriously. What changes in our understanding, and in us, when we see God as a friend, not as an irritated judge or distant monarch, who whispers wisdom to us in a loving concern to help us amend ourselves? Second, is this a poem just about the need for a more simplistic honesty when writing about God or is it also suggestive of how our lives need a cleansing from pretensions and deceptions and the bustle of competitiveness and distraction? What would happen if a life tried only to *copie out* love a bit better so that, in between its lines of pain and beauty, God may be glorified in a distilled and simpler soul? As Herbert writes in his poem 'A Wreath', 'Give me simplicitie, that I may live.'

The Quip

The merrie world did on a day
With his train-bands and mates agree
To meet together, where I lay,
And all in sport to jeer at me.

First, Beautie crept into a rose,
Which when I pluckt not, Sir, said she,
Tell me, I pray, Whose hands are those?
But thou shalt answer, Lord, for me.

Then Money came, and chinking still,
What tune is this, poore man? said he:
I heard in Musick you had skill.
But thou shalt answer, Lord, for me.

Then came brave Glorie puffing by
In silks that whistled, who but he?
He scarce allow'd me half an eie.
But thou shalt answer, Lord, for me.

Then came quick Wit and Conversation,
And he would needs a comfort be,
And, to be short, make an oration.
But thou shalt answer, Lord, for me.

Yet when the houre of thy designe
To answer these fine things shall come;
Speak not at large, say, I am thine:
And then they have their answer home.

A quip is a sharp remark, often aimed at a person to put him or her down. In this poem, in which we have a sort of beauty parade of the world's posturing or, as one critic puts it, a 'brief processional masque of Worldly Delight' (Vendler, 1975, p. 184), we find that the quips are fired by them at Herbert. He has a quip too. It is not, however, a bullet-like sarcasm, but a quip in the other meaning of the word: a wise saying. This takes the form of his refrain to the Lord, that *thou shalt answer, Lord, for me*.

The poem begins by telling us that, one day, the *merrie world* called together its soldiers and friends to meet where Herbert lay. Metaphorically this might be his inner life, his soul. Bullies always tell us that they are only joking and, here, they assemble to have a bit of sport with Herbert. *Beautie* is the first to have a go, creeping into a beautiful flower that, when he doesn't pluck it, asks him, *Whose hands are those?* That is, can you really be so dumb as to not be enticed by what's on offer? By making the flower a *rose*, an emblem of female beauty, Herbert leads us to see this dialogue as about more than horticulture.

Money then appears, *chinking* his coins. Because Herbert is not interested in him, Money says that he is out of tune with the world, naive and therefore *poore*. Money thinks Herbert is skilful at music, but obviously not in the music of real people, the music that makes us all dance to its anxious tune. Then *brave* (well-dressed) *Glorie* comes puffing by, swollen with reputation and hot air. His clothes of silk whistle as they move. We know from Herbert's early biographer that the young Herbert rather liked his clothes and this may be some spiritual stocktaking at work as he recognizes his weaknesses, past and present. Whereas Herbert is taking a good look at himself, *Glorie* can hardly be bothered to cast him *half an eie.*

Wit and Conversation is next on the scene, insisting that he is not like the others and will, instead, be a comfort and will make an oration. Herbert had been Public Orator at the University of Cambridge and knew the devices and exaggerations of public speaking. You sense that, in the presence of this worldly being, Herbert can't get a word in edgeways and will not be listened to or found to be of interest. Wit seeks its own rewards and rarely bothers about others. So, as with all the others who have ridiculed him, Herbert holds fast to the hope that the Lord will answer on his behalf.

The poem ends with a request to God. Herbert asks that, when the time comes for some accountability by the world for its self-admiring and hurtful ways, God will not say much and will not be like a judge delivering a long summing up speech in court. He just wants God to say, *I am thine.* It doesn't matter whether God or Herbert is the subject of this sentence because the outcome is the same: they belong together and they are as one. To have their *answer home* means to get the answer that ends the conversation because it 'strikes home'; it is the final word on the matter.

It has been said that today we live in a circle of spending money we don't have on things we don't want in order to impress people we don't like. It was ever thus. Herbert's world, similarly, revolved around surface appeal, getting rich, pursuing a name for oneself and being able to use language in such a way that put you in charge or on top. Herbert knew this world only too well, as do we. When we lie on that last hospital bed, however, none of this will mean anything. We will just want to know that *I am thine* and that I always was and will be.

Dialogue

Sweetest Saviour, if my soul
     Were but worth the having,
Quickly should I then controll
     Any thought of waving.
But when all my care and pains
Cannot give the name of gains
To thy wretch so full of stains;
What delight or hope remains?

What (childe) is the ballance thine,
     Thine the poise and measure?
If I say, Thou shalt be mine;
     Finger not my treasure.
What the gains in having thee
Do amount to, onely he,
Who for man was sold, can see;
That transferr'd th' accounts to me.

But as I can see no merit,
     Leading to this favour:
So the way to fit me for it,
     Is beyond my savour.
As the reason then is thine;
So the way is none of mine:

I disclaim the whole designe:
Sinne disclaims and I resigne.

That is all, if that I could
Get without repining;
And my clay my creature would
Follow my resigning.
That as I did freely part
With my glorie and desert,
Left all joyes to feel all smart ----
Ah! no more: thou break'st my heart.

In some ways this poem can be seen as a harbinger to Herbert's poem 'Love (III)', in which a similar dialogue between Christ and Herbert takes place as to whether or not Herbert is worthy enough to be loved. This dialogue is part of a long tradition found, for instance, in the poetry of the Hebrew Scriptures, where two-voiced intimate conversations between the Creator and the created often clarify the nature of their relationship. Such dialogues were also popular in seventeenth-century poetry.

Herbert begins by telling his *Sweetest Saviour* that if he believed his soul was worth having, he would control any thought he had of *waving*, disclaiming, his salvation. The similarity of this word to 'wavering', with its overtones of uncertainty and dithering, add to the sense Herbert conveys. But because he is so full of *care and pains* and *full of stains*, he realizes that he isn't worth gaining, and so *What delight or hope remains?*

Christ replies by calling Herbert *childe* and then asking if Herbert is the one who balances the books or holds the scales. If, says Christ, I say you shall be mine, don't start meddling with my treasure! As is the case with love, it is only the one who loves who understands the depths of what the beloved one means to them. So here, Christ, and *onely he*, knows the worth of the poet. He was worth so much that he was sold for him and had all of Herbert's debts *transferr'd* to him.

Herbert comes back at Christ and says he can see no merit in himself that deserves this, and knowing how to earn such love is beyond him. The reason and way of proceeding is Christ's alone and Herbert says he just has to *disclaim the whole designe* and *resigne*. Here, 'resign' can mean either that Herbert resigns himself to not meriting redemption or he simply surrenders and yields to Christ. Herbert probably means the first, while Christ hears the second.

The last stanza is Christ's response to Herbert's paralysing shame and self-doubt. It is good to stop struggling or *repining*, complaining, against love's way and follow his own example of resigning when he came to earth and lived a life for God by putting off his *glorie*, leaving his *joyes* and feeling such *smart*, searing pain. At this point we have the extraordinary, breathless moment when Herbert breaks in to stop Christ saying anything more. He can't bear to hear about what Christ went through: *Ah! no more: thou break'st my heart.* The poem leads us from a complex web of both false and genuine pride and humility on Herbert's part to the wide and transparent space of Christ's pure, and undeserved, gift of love that, in the end, no words can express. All words have to eventually dissolve in the presence of God.

Throughout the dialogue, Herbert wants to make a point and Christ wants to make a difference. Herbert is right to see that the heart of the human problem is the problem of the human heart, but what he doesn't understand at first is that the heart cannot be healed by itself; it needs love from outside itself. It needs tender care and touching back into life. This saving act, of showing us we are loveable by loving us to the point we just don't understand and wonder if it can be true, is the healing work of incarnation. It is a dialogue of renovating, restoring, intimate friendship and hope.

Hope

I gave to Hope a watch of mine: but he
        An anchor gave to me.
Then an old prayer-book I did present:
        And he an optick sent.
With that I gave a viall full of tears:
        But he a few green eares:
Ah Loyterer! I'le no more, no more I'le bring:
        I did expect a ring.

When Herbert's contemporary John Donne was ordained, he adopted a seal with a particular design on it: Christ crucified on an anchor. Not long before he died, Donne is said to have had copies of the seal made to be sent to the friends he valued most. These included Herbert who, in gratitude, wrote a poem in Latin to Donne exploring the image.

'Hope' is another poem by Herbert that includes reference to an anchor. He uses it as the first gift that Hope, who is a personification of Christ here, gives to him. With its cruciform shape, and with words from the letter to the Hebrews in mind, that 'the hope set before us' is 'an anchor of the soul, both sure and steadfast' (6.18–19), it is an emblem for one of the three Christian virtues that sometimes gets overlooked. It is given to Herbert in response to his gift of *a watch*. Is this Herbert mistakenly thinking that hope is time-bound? Is it a present that is stuck in the present while hope looks patiently ahead? Or maybe the watch, a human mechanism with hands that seek to contain each moment, falsely embodies the idea that hope is human in origin and not of God, eternal in source and scope?

Herbert then gives another gift – an *old prayer-book*. This is a symbol of his devotion through life, in all its turbulence and peacefulness. In return, Hope gives him a telescope, an *optick*, through which great things can be seen from a distance. Hope has a heavenly origin and can be made effective not simply by reciting prayers but by dedicated attention to the long view and a willingness to work and act in such a way that it is brought nearer to this world in the same way that a telescope brings distant realities into our living rooms.

Like the psalmist who stored up his tears in a bottle (Psalm 56.8), Herbert then hands over the tears he has shed in this frustrating give and take with Hope. Are they tears of penitence? Of anger, at himself or at God? Maybe tears of loneliness and hopelessness? Tears resist abstract intellectual reasoning: they come from a deep, dark, often unexplored place. Some Christian writers have spoken of the 'gift of tears' as not only an honest offering to God but a gift to the self as they cleanse the soul into a more immediate and transparent expression of itself. Hope seems to recognize the potential of this gift and in return offers *a few green eares*, promising a harvest.

Herbert now loses it and barks out his irritation. He calls Hope a *Loyterer*, someone who delays giving, because he has offered his time, reverence and penitence and still hasn't had what he expected in return for them – *a ring*. He has wanted full union, a covenant, a ring that speaks of for ever, and all that came his way was a seeming postponement. Why has Hope never proposed? The courtship nature of this lyric becomes especially noticeable. Hope, it seems, never domesticates and settles down. The complete spiritual union between Christ and the person of faith is necessarily a restless longing and the pulse of faith.

St Augustine famously said that Hope has two beautiful daughters: Anger (at the ways things are) and Courage (to put them right). Both of them are brought into this world by the confidence but not the certainty of Hope. Martin Luther King Jr never said, 'I have a nightmare,' even though he had many in his time. He said that he had a dream and it was being motivated only by this hope that enabled him to help people reimagine the world and to pray for God's will to be done on earth as it is in heaven. Hope is a soul's strong but deep down, unseen, anchor.

Sinnes Round

Sorrie I am, my God, sorrie I am,
That my offences course it in a ring.
My thoughts are working like a busie flame,
Untill their cockatrice they hatch and bring:
And when they once have perfected their draughts,
My words take fire from my inflamed thoughts.

My words take fire from my inflamed thoughts,
Which spit it forth like the Sicilian hill.
They vent the wares, and passe them with their faults,
And by their breathing ventilate the ill.
But words suffice not, where are lewd intentions:
My hands do joyn to finish the inventions.

My hands do joyn to finish the inventions:
And so my sinnes ascend three stories high,
As Babel grew, before there were dissensions.
Yet ill deeds loyter not: for they supplie
New thoughts of sinning: wherefore, to my shame,
Sorrie I am, my God, sorrie I am.

When I was young, I learned to play the recorder at school and we seemed to spend a lot of time playing 'rounds', each player playing the tune in turn and with an overlap so that it never ended – until the teacher told us to stop. This meaning of the word 'round', coupled with that of it also being a circle dance, expresses Herbert's view of sin being repetitious, compulsive and self-perpetuating. There is something inherently circular about sin – its phrasing hauntingly enticing to others, yet having no purpose except its own self-referential notation.

'Sinnes Round' is a penitential prayer, each stanza focusing in turn on sins of thought, word and deed. The circularity of sin is stated in the second line. Herbert's thoughts then work like a *busie flame*, scorching himself and others in all their heat. The *cockatrice* most probably refers to an alchemy myth of the day, it being a fiery serpent creature hatched in a cockerel's egg and portrayed with its tail in its mouth, feeding on itself. Our thoughts can create a reality well removed from what is real, yet our words come from this internal world of our own frenzied, emotional and fearful making. Herbert knows that his words are not kind when they originate in a tortured mind. 'Out of the abundance of the heart the mouth speaketh', taught Jesus (Matthew 12.34).

Picking up the refrain at the end of the first stanza, the second stanza continues the round. Herbert reflects on how his words can spew and spit like Mount Etna. His words do their unpleasant work, emitting his faults with them and fanning the flames of ill will. But, as if this weren't enough, his low and lascivious words couple up with his hands to finish the inventions, to complete the devices and desires of his own heart.

Sin builds on itself. With thoughts that turn to words that turn to action, it constructs an edifice in a life, like the Babel tower, that tries to compete with heaven and those things that come from there – truth, beauty, justice, faith, peace. Herbert shows the circle of sin again at the end of the poem. His actions are not the end of the matter. They instead *supplie/New thoughts of sinning* and so the whole sorrowful tale begins again. The poem ends where it began – or did it begin where it ended? *Sorrie I am, my God, sorrie I am.*

Herbert's poem is a timely reminder that the things which matter most in life – trust, love, compassion, kindness, courage – all increase as we share them. Unlike money and power, where if I win you lose, these enable others to win if we do. They increase and cannot be contained or hoarded. Pursue one of these and life will improve for more than just you. In contrast, to sin means to live a life curved in on itself, feeding on its own poisons and leaking acids over those who unhappily find themselves close by. It is a circle that needs to be broken. Recognition is the first step of salvation. To say *sorrie* is the second.

It is said that, to keep a relationship alive, it is necessary to learn to keep saying, as the years go by, three things: 'I'm sorry', 'I forgive you' and 'I love you'. In Herbert's poetry, these things are said time and time again in his relationship with God, by both, as God and he, with their honeymoon well over, seek to live together in an honest and stable partnership that still has plenty of room for surprise and growth. His love for God, beautifully full of joy and hope, will always mean, from time to time, taking a proper and responsible look at himself and saying, *Sorrie I am, my God, sorrie I am.*

Gratefulnesse

Thou that hast giv'n so much to me,
Give one thing more, a gratefull heart.
See how thy beggar works on thee
                              By art.

He makes thy gifts occasion more,
And sayes, If he in this be crost,
All thou hast giv'n him heretofore
                              Is lost.

But thou didst reckon, when at first
Thy word our hearts and hands did crave,
What it would come to at the worst
                              To save.

Perpetuall knockings at thy doore,
Tears sullying thy transparent rooms,
Gift upon gift, much would have more,
                              And comes.

This not withstanding, thou wentst on,
And didst allow us all our noise:
Nay thou hast made a sigh and grone
                              Thy joyes.

Not that thou hast not still above
Much better tunes, then grones can make;
But that these countrey-aires thy love
                Did take.

Wherefore I crie, and crie again;
And in no quiet canst thou be,
Till I a thankfull heart obtain
                Of thee:

Not thankfull, when it pleaseth me;
As if thy blessings had spare dayes:
But such a heart, whose pulse may be
                Thy praise.

'If the only prayer you ever say in your life is "Thank you", that will be enough.' This saying is often attributed to the medieval mystic and theologian Meister Eckhart. The Eucharist, which lies at the heart of Christian life and prayer, means the service of 'thanksgiving'. Jesus was astounded that only one out of ten lepers healed from their disease returned to give thanks (Luke 17.11–19). The ancient Assyrians had a word for prayer that was also used for the act of opening a clenched fist. Instead of prayer being seen as a demanding activity where a gripped fist is banged on the table, prayer was understood by them as an opening up of life in gratitude for what is placed in our hands. St Kevin was said to hold his hands open so long in prayer that a blackbird nested and hatched her young in them. Despite all these stories reminding us that thankfulness is the foundation of a Christian life, practising such thankfulness can be hard. As Herbert knew, it is something we need to pray for.

In this somewhat overlooked poem, Herbert tells God that he has been given so much in life, but he needs one thing more, *a gratefull heart*. To be grateful means being more attentive, taking nothing for granted, being willing to place another's praise before your own. Under pressure and in a world where many of us have such a strong sense of entitlement, such gratefulness can be rare and difficult. Picking up a saying of John Calvin's, that when we pray we should adopt the mind of a beggar, Herbert says he works on God to help him improve.

To be grateful for gifts in life means you recognize more of them, but, says Herbert in the second stanza, if his prayer for thankfulness isn't accepted, or is *crost*, even what he has been given will be wasted by being unseen or met with indifference. God knew, he continues, what he was taking on when he asked for our hearts and hands. He knew that we would keep knocking on his door and sharing our tears and heartache. Herbert then appears to refer to Matthew 13.12: 'For whosoever hath, to him shall be given, and he shall have more abundance.'

God does not turn us away. He allows us *all our noise*, and our sighs and groans become his joys because, through such honest expression, the relationship with his people is not shaped by pretence, falsity or self-affirmation, but is real and ready for change and growth. Herbert suggests that God prefers to listen to the rustic and unsophisticated *countrey-aires* of human beings than the better tunes of the heavenly choirs.

The penultimate stanza shows Herbert to be rather bullying of God, like the persistent widow (Luke 18.1–8) who won't give up until she gets what she's asking for. God can be in *no quiet* because of this and won't be until Herbert has that grateful heart. He ends by clarifying what it is he wants: not a heart that manages to remember to say 'thank you' when it pleases him, as if some days went by without much to be grateful for and *blessings had spare dayes*, but a healthy heart whose beat is consistent praise. In his poem 'Praise (II)' he proclaims that he will praise God 'Sev'n whole dayes, not one in seven'.

There's a humour in this poem, a lightness of touch in Herbert's appreciation of the irony of bullying God to become more grateful. It is touching too as we see ourselves outlined so vividly. Which of us could not pray the fresh opening two lines with an equally urgent need?

> Thou that hast giv'n so much to me,
> Give one thing more, a gratefull heart.

The Holdfast

I threatned to observe the strict decree
        Of my deare God with all my power & might.
        But I was told by one, it could not be;
Yet I must trust in God to be my light.

Then will I trust, said I, in him alone.
        Nay, ev'n to trust in him, was also his:
        We must confesse, that nothing is our own.
Then I confesse that he my succour is:

But to have nought is ours, not to confesse
        That we have nought. I stood amaz'd at this,
        Much troubled, till I heard a friend expresse,
That all things were more ours by being his.
        What Adam had, and forfeited for all,
        Christ keepeth now, who cannot fail or fall.

A holdfast is a lock that supports and holds together a building. It can also refer to a persistent or self-motivating person and, for those who read the Scriptures, it has a resonance with Paul's first letter to the Thessalonians, when he tells them to 'hold fast that which is good' (5.21). As usual with Herbert, all these come into play through the poem. We get the image of Christ being the chief cornerstone (1 Peter 2.6) at the end of the poem, the one we must hold fast to. But also, throughout the poem, the poet is rather self-assertive and seeks to control the situation. Count up the number of times *I* is used. The poet tries to take charge of the poem at first, but gradually disappears at the end.

The sonnet begins with the poet announcing that he *threatned,* or vowed strictly, to observe the laws of God – presumably to love God and neighbour. The focus appears to be more on the poet, though. The first word is *I* and we hear of *my power & might* and even *my . . . God.* Someone tells him, however, that this is not possible on his terms and, instead of asserting his own power in his relationship with God, it is better to trust God to be his light. A spiritual shift takes place. Instead of the poet being in charge of his discipleship, something he motivates and shapes, he is invited to accept God as his *light.* It is not, as it were, his own understanding that he must trust, but that which his understanding must learn to be changed by – God.

The poet concedes and says that he will trust then and surrender some control. Whoever his conversation partner is here tells him that not even this is feasible, because trusting God must be welcomed as a gift, not as an achievement. When it comes to God, nothing is our own; all is a reckless outpouring of generosity that we have to learn to receive into empty hands. One commentator sums up the poem as believing that 'every grace is the gift of God, even the grace to acknowledge our gracelessness' (Summers, 1954, p. 61). Or, in Herbert's words, *to have nought is ours, not to confesse/That we have nought.*

The poet tells us that he *stood amaz'd* at all this and was *much troubled.* There certainly is a tone of negativity in the air from what the person is telling him. It feels as if, when it comes to God, we are nothing and nothing we can do or say adds up to much, so we had better learn to be passive. Then there comes an intervention from a friend who tells him that, on the contrary, all things were *more ours by being his*. Our surrender to God is our freedom. Our emptiness is our fullness. Our weakness is our strength – all because life's foundation is God and not our own prejudices or spiritual pride. What Adam had, he lost, because he couldn't trust himself. The last word of the poem ominously reminds us of this and of our common humanity with him. Now, though, Christ is our holdfast, not ourselves, and it is his fidelity towards us, not ours towards him, that is the Christian hope.

The post-resurrection stories in the Gospels express this hope. Christ comes to the forlorn disciples, who are full of guilt and remorse for how they ran away and denied knowing him, and he turns up in the places he had been with them. He reminds them of their relationship, how it all began, how it once flourished, but how, in the end, they walked away. He comes to them to say 'shalom' or 'peace', with a day-to-day meaning more like 'hi'. He shows them that it is his love for them now that will be their strength to carry on and begin their work again as apostles. They know what they are capable of, but they know his love is greater and won't give up on them. They are learning too that all things are *more ours by being his.*

Praise (II)

King of Glorie, King of Peace,
        I will love thee:
And that love may never cease,
        I will move thee.

Thou hast granted my request,
        Thou hast heard me:
Thou didst note my working breast,
        Thou hast spar'd me.

Wherefore with my utmost art
        I will sing thee,
And the cream of all my heart
        I will bring thee.

Though my sinnes against me cried,
        Thou didst cleare me;
And alone, when they replied,
        Thou didst heare me.

Sev'n whole dayes, not one in seven,
        I will praise thee.
In my heart, though not in heaven,
        I can raise thee.

Thou grew'st soft and moist with tears,
Thou relentedst:
And when Justice call'd for fears,
Thou dissentedst.

Small it is, in this poore sort
To enroll thee:
Ev'n eternitie is too short
To extoll thee.

This is the second of three poems that Herbert entitled
'Praise'. Each tends to give voice to the need to honour
and celebrate the being of God, and the outpouring of
God's love in creation, while at the same time admitting
how awkward and inappropriate we are when we set about
trying to do this. This poem is better-known than many
of Herbert's poems because it is often sung as a popular
hymn. It has been much appreciated by critics. T. S. Eliot,
for instance, applauded its 'masterly simplicity' (1962, p. 33)
and others have similarly enjoyed its low-key ingenuity. In
many ways, it is Herbert's attempt at a psalm. It weaves
in phrases found in the Psalms and pursues its own style of
Hebrew parallelism of sounds and images.

God is first addressed as *King of Glorie* and *King of Peace*.
For those who would make God a convenient holy support to
human glory, often acquired by the shedding of blood or the
humiliation of others, the corrective is found here that God is
also peaceful and the God of all people, not just of the biggest
armies or egos. In typical Herbert monosyllables, he then says
quite simply that *I will love thee*. And so that God's love will
never stop, he also says that he will *move*, or appeal, to God

continually. He says that God has granted his *request* by hearing his *working breast*. This refers to prayers that come from the conflicted heart and not the rational head.

Herbert tells God that, because of this, he will use all his artistry in word and music to praise him as he deserves. He will offer *the cream*, the best part, of his heart. Herbert is aware of his sins as he prays. They cry against him like the blood of Abel cried against Cain (Genesis 4.10), but God settles the debt. *Alone*, when he is still tormented by the past, God bears with him and hears, soothes, forgives. We live at a permanent crossroads, the point where a past that has affected us and a future which lies open to us meet together in the present. God's loyalty is to the future, not to the past.

Herbert is committed to praising God each day and not just on a Sunday. He can *raise* God, praise him, in his heart, but he cannot control God. He knows that God is not a God of revenge and cruelty, but is *soft* and has *tears* of pain when those he loves suffer or press their self-destruct buttons in self-hate. When they have failed to love, and justice would call them to order and fearfully declare a verdict, God instead steps down from the judge's seat and embraces us in the dock.

It is a small thing in the light of eternity for a human being to honour, *enroll*, God. In fact, concludes Herbert, eternity itself is *too short* to magnify God. We don't use the word 'magnify' much these days, except when thinking of magnifying glasses that make things look bigger. This is what praise of God ultimately seeks to do. True praise makes God bigger, more discernible to us, in our lives, in the Church, in the world. Humans tend to start to resemble what they worship in life but, by magnifying God, we simply seek to make God, and not ourselves, the centre of our hearts and minds and wills. We seek to deepen our relationship with God in the only way possible – love. Herbert's poem began by praying that *love may never cease*. Love, Herbert believed, is the sole spiritual imperative and the only law of the authentic soul.

The Collar

I struck the board, and cry'd, No more.
                                    I will abroad.
What? shall I ever sigh and pine?
My lines and life are free; free as the rode,
        Loose as the winde, as large as store.
                Shall I be still in suit?
Have I no harvest but a thorn
To let me bloud, and not restore
What I have lost with cordiall fruit?
                                    Sure there was wine
            Before my sighs did drie it: there was corn
            Before my tears did drown it.
        Is the yeare onely lost to me?
                Have I no bayes to crown it?
No flowers, no garlands gay? all blasted?
                                    All wasted?
        Not so, my heart: but there is fruit,
                        And thou hast hands.
            Recover all thy sigh-blown age
On double pleasures: leave thy cold dispute
Of what is fit, and not forsake thy cage,
                        Thy rope of sands,
Which pettie thoughts have made, and made to thee
        Good cable, to enforce and draw,
                        And be thy law,

> While thou didst wink and wouldst not see.
>> Away; take heed:
>> I will abroad.
> Call in thy deaths head there: tie up thy fears.
>> He that forbears
>> To suit and serve his need,
>>> Deserves his load.
> But as I rav'd and grew more fierce and wilde
>> At every word,
>> Me thoughts I heard one calling, *Childe*:
>>> And I reply'd, *My Lord*.

Herbert had a good ear for the sounds of words. The title of this poem, 'The Collar', is a little puzzling. Does the collar suggest imprisonment, restriction or ownership? Or does it refer to Christ's easy yoke (Matthew 11.29–30)? Are we meant to hear other words in it, such as 'caller'? Herbert calls out in the poem and God calls to him at the end of it, when Herbert calms down into a restored sense of his 'calling'. Or can we hear the word 'choler'? This was thought to be the 'humour' that made one irascible and hot-headed, which Herbert is in the poem. In fact, his brother Edward once wrote of George that 'he was not exempt from passion and choler, being infirmities to which all our race is subject' (1888, p. 12). It appears to be a triple pun that reveals the poem's multifaceted insights on what has been called the 'warfare of the will' (Halewood, 1970, p. 90). Herbert can't live with God and can't live without God. The tension creates and shapes his soul.

It begins with the poet banging *the board*, which, in his time, referred to a table but also, more specifically, to the altar in a church. He has had enough and says he's off. The chaotic form of the poem at this point indicates his internal state of mind. He decides that he is *free as the rode* (note the similarity of the word *rode* to 'rood', Christ's cross), although the freedom he envisages is the secular understanding of simply being free to do or be anything he wants, whereas the freedom spoken of in the Gospel has the compass of truth attached, because truth, ultimately, is what makes us free (John 8.32). But Herbert doesn't want to hear all that at the moment. He's having a late adolescent fit and just wants to escape! *Shall I be still in suit?* he asks. Is he always to be petitioning and subservient? Again, the question has another meaning. Can Herbert be still when he is not the one in charge? Or will he always be restless and in revolt when he feels he lacks liberty?

Have I no harvest but a thorn . . . ? In Milton's *Paradise Lost*, we are told that, before the Fall, the rose was 'without thorn' (2003, iv 256) and Herbert's whirlpool of emotion feels as if it is part of a disordered world in freefall, where what has been lost is not restored but the loss simply put up with. He has had *wine* and *corn*, but life has taken away their pleasures. These are, of course, the elements of the Eucharist, where, back on the board, what has been lost and restored is celebrated and offered to God in gratitude. But Herbert's life feels *lost* to him, like a vase of dead flowers. Is it *all wasted?* he asks in angry lament.

Then the other side of his brain has its say and starts to correct his despairing thoughts. He reminds himself that he has a will and it is now time to *Recover all thy sigh-blown age/ On double pleasures.* He rejects the cold dispute of doctrinal differences and academic arrogance ('*Disputandi pruritus, scabies ecclesiae*' – 'The itch of disputing is the scab of the Church' – is how Sir Henry Wooton is said to have put it).

These are a *rope of sands*, an ultimately fruitless exercise. *Pettie thoughts* became law and he wouldn't see it, but lived in a cage he mistook for life. He is resolved and says it again: *I will abroad.*

You can almost feel him packing his bags as he tells himself to *call in thy deaths head* and remember his mortality. He's only got one life, so why waste it? If people want to shackle themselves up well, they deserve their *load*. His play on what we deserve when we de-serve is yet another poignant pun. Herbert whips himself into a storm: *I rav'd and grew more fierce and wilde.* Yet, even as his words get hotter, expressive of a tortured soul, the more resolute they sound, the less you believe them. Rather like a parent who has spent time listening to a teenager shout and complain, God eventually steps in and reminds Herbert that he is his *childe* and to ask if he has finished moaning yet, because there's a whole day to be enjoyed together when he stops. It's like God saying, 'Yes, I've heard all that. Now, back to business.' Some may find this too controlling and wonder whether Herbert has a point, but the end of the poem reminds me of Jesus' encounter with Mary Magdalene at the tomb when she is simply called back to herself, to tearful hope, by Jesus tenderly saying her name.

The poem ends with Herbert answering, maybe with a blush, *My Lord*. Like Thomas, the disciple who doubted, he recognizes the voice of the one he first loved and followed and who even now, in the midst of such hurt and confused thoughts, is still there, loving, unable to abandon us to our tendency to damage ourselves. God calls us out – seeing us as we are and drawing us out of where we are. If we are to stay with him, he doesn't seek our certainty but our confidence.

The Call

Come, my Way, my Truth, my Life:
Such a Way, as gives us breath:
Such a Truth, as ends all strife:
And such a Life, as killeth death.

Come, my Light, my Feast, my Strength:
Such a Light, as shows a feast:
Such a Feast, as mends in length:
Such a Strength, as makes his guest.

Come, my Joy, my Love, my Heart:
Such a Joy, as none can move:
Such a Love, as none can part:
Such a Heart, as joyes in love.

This poem is almost entirely crafted from words of one syllable. Only the word *killeth* interrupts the pattern. There is a simplicity to its tone, but a complexity in its interlacing of ideas. It is rich in biblical reference and, as has been pointed out by critics, it takes absolute nouns that refer to God and points to how they descend into the reality of the world and play their transforming part. In this poem, words become incarnate as they confidently call out to the Word, who became incarnate.

Deep in the heart of Christian faith is a sacred hunger. We learn through life that we are incomplete and don't seem able, ultimately, to heal ourselves. This means that we are prompted to look out of ourselves and invoke the One who creates, upholds and redeems our every moment, praying with longing that we might distil our defences and make space for God so that grace might do its work in and through us. Christian faith is a religion in the vocative. It invokes God to come and touch us back into life. This poem captures something of this restless hope in a tightly contained and economical form.

Jesus, in John's Gospel, tells his listeners that he is the way, the truth and the life (14.6). Here, Herbert makes them *my* way, truth and life. He personalizes them and shows that these words live only if there is a strong and loving pulse in the faith of the one who claims them. Christ as his *Way* does not make him breathless, as many journeys do but, rather, gives us breath. Instead of truth being something we fight and fall out over, Christ as *Truth* comes as peace and nurse. As *Life*, he is a God of endless beginnings and endless fidelity and so *killeth death*. Or, as John Donne writes in a holy sonnet (10), 'Death, thou shalt die.'

Jesus also speaks of himself as the light of the world (John 8.12) and the living bread (John 6.51). Herbert probably uses the word *Feast* instead of 'bread' to evoke the communal aspect of Christ's nourishment – his invitation to everyone to belong, participate and celebrate, not just those who think they own the menu. The Feast *mends in length* – that is, improves as it goes on, like the wedding at Cana (John 2.1–11). Christ is the *Strength* that makes us all his guests against all the odds.

Although we can forget the fact very quickly, God is love (1 John 4.16), and Herbert makes the last verse a call to the one who has captured his heart. Jonathan Swift said that we usually have just enough religion to hate one another, but not enough religion to love one another. Herbert unashamedly ends his poem with an immersion in the vocabulary of love. No one can take away his joy; nothing can separate him from God's love. The last line reminds us that Christ has joy when love is celebrated and made the true meaning in a life. He is *my Heart* that *joyes in love*. Herbert wants to live this truth, not just give voice to it. He calls to Christ, like the last pages of the Bible, to come to him (Revelation 22.20). The last line of this verse repeats some of the words of the first line, giving a sense of the completeness of love, that wholeness for which the whole poem aches.

This poem beautifully exemplifies Martin Luther's belief that prayer is not overcoming God's reluctance but laying hold of his willingness. It gives us another refreshing glimpse into Herbert's soul and the God he craved to love more.

The Pulley

When God at first made man,
Having a glasse of blessings standing by;
Let us (said he) poure on him all we can:
Let the worlds riches, which dispersed lie,
Contract into a span.

So strength first made a way;
Then beautie flow'd, then wisdome, honour, pleasure:
When almost all was out, God made a stay,
Perceiving that alone of all his treasure
Rest in the bottome lay.

For if I should (said he)
Bestow this jewell also on my creature,
He would adore my gifts in stead of me,
And rest in Nature, not the God of Nature:
So both should losers be.

Yet let him keep the rest,
But keep them with repining restlesnesse:
Let him be rich and wearie, that at least,
If goodnesse leade him not, yet wearinesse
May tosse him to my breast.

The Pulley

The book of Genesis opens with God at the beginning of creation looking at all the life he has brought into being and saying how good it is. God's creation was full of both diversity and blessing. In a rather jaunty tone, Herbert takes us back to that moment but, daringly, presents his own bold take on what happened when it came to making human beings. It is an inversion of the Greek myth of Pandora's jar, where all the evils of the world are let out of it except hope, whose comfort remains, though surrounded by pained and distorted existence. Here, though, God bestows good things on humanity, but decides to keep rest from them so that human beings remain restless, their sense of incompleteness then prompting them to understand their need for God.

Herbert was an admirer of St Augustine and it is easy to see how the saint's thoughts influenced this poem. John Burnaby has commented that at the heart of Augustine's understanding of the love of God is *desiderium* – 'the unsatisfied longing of the homesick heart' (2007, p. 96). Or, in Augustine's own words (1995, p. 179):

> The whole life of the good Christian is a holy longing.
> What you long for, as yet you do not see ... by withholding
> of the vision God extends the longing, through longing
> he extends the soul, by extending it he makes room in
> it ... So let us long, because we are to be filled ... That is
> our life, to be exercised by longing.

The title of the poem refers to a mechanical device that moves heavy cargo by way of ropes and wheels. By pulling down on the end of one rope, something is pulled upwards on the other. So, as we are pulled down by our *restlesnesse*, so we are at the same time raised nearer to God. The titles of two recent books make a similar point: Richard Rohr's *Falling Upward* (SPCK, 2013) and Alice Oswald's collection of poems *Falling Awake* (Jonathan Cape, 2016). The parable told by Jesus of the prodigal son always comes to my mind when I read this poem. The moment the son sees where his chaotic and confused life has got him, he turns to go home, working out what he's going to say. Then, as he turns round, he sees his dad beaming and waving, jogging down the road towards him – that is the pulley in action.

In this poem, the world's riches all contract into a human life. These riches are physical and social, from *beautie* to *honour*, but down at the bottom of the box lies *rest*. Herbert always enjoys good wordplay and, in this case, 'rest' refers not only to repose but also to what remains; so in the last verse, when God says let him keep the rest, he does so even as he decides that they should not have rest! God decides not to hand over rest in case people learn to rest in it. A sense of complete wholeness would mean that we see only ourselves and not our dependence. So God decides that we should be *rich and wearie*, have lots to live with but are always in search of what to live for. He makes us people of *repining restlesnesse*, and you can hear the pining, the longing lament, within that repining.

Herbert tells us that God made a *stay*. This can mean that God stopped pouring out his blessings: we feel our un-finished reality each day. 'Stay' can also refer to a support, something we hold on to that keeps us steady and upright. The two meanings meet each other and enrich what Herbert considers to be a spiritual truth about our relationship to the world, to ourselves and to God. The disquiet that leads to the soul's quietness, a weariness that is our only hope, the withheld blessing that becomes the most treasured blessing of all – all these ironies and jostling feelings, from dereliction to devotion, make for a restlessness in Herbert's poetry that edges us nearer God. His poems continually help us hear the freshness of Christ's words: 'Come unto me, all ye that labour and are heavy laden, and I will give you rest' (Matthew 11.28).

The Flower

How fresh, O Lord, how sweet and clean
Are thy returns! ev'n as the flowers in spring;
    To which, besides their own demean,
The late-past frosts tributes of pleasure bring.
        Grief melts away
        Like snow in May,
As if there were no such cold thing.

Who would have thought my shrivel'd heart
Could have recover'd greennesse? It was gone
    Quite under ground; as flowers depart
To see their mother-root, when they have blown;
        Where they together
        All the hard weather,
Dead to the world, keep house unknown.

These are thy wonders, Lord of power,
Killing and quickning, bringing down to hell
    And up to heaven in an houre;
Making a chiming of a passing-bell.
        We say amisse,
        This or that is:
Thy word is all, if we could spell.

The Flower

O that I once past changing were,
Fast in thy Paradise, where no flower can wither!
Many a spring I shoot up fair,
Offring at heav'n, growing and groaning thither:
             Nor doth my flower
             Want a spring-showre,
My sinnes and I joining together:

But while I grow in a straight line,
Still upwards bent, as if heav'n were mine own,
Thy anger comes, and I decline:
What frost to that? what pole is not the zone,
             Where all things burn,
             When thou dost turn,
And the least frown of thine is shown?

And now in age I bud again,
After so many deaths I live and write;
I once more smell the dew and rain,
And relish versing: O my onely light,
             It cannot be
             That I am he
On whom thy tempests fell all night.

These are thy wonders, Lord of love,
To make us see we are but flowers that glide:
Which when we once can finde and prove,
Thou hast a garden for us, where to bide.
             Who would be more,
             Swelling through store,
Forfeit their Paradise by their pride.

The poet Coleridge said in a letter of 1826 that the poetry of George Herbert helped him with his 'tendency to self-contempt' (1887, pp. 248–9). He particularly liked this poem, calling it 'delicious' and 'especially affecting' (Patrides, 1983, pp. 166–73). He is not alone in his admiration. Critics have hailed 'The Flower' as one of the finest lyrics in the language, praising its combination of order and surprise. It is one of the most popular of Herbert's poems placed in anthologies and it has a very complex form. The poem has a vivid freshness to it even though its subject is serious. This is helped by the couplets near the end of each verse and the rhyming words at the end of lines 2, 4 and 7 – giving a satisfying sense of completion to each verse and to the whole.

In one of the Genesis creation stories (Genesis 1), humankind is made by God on the sixth of seven days. In this poem, it is in the sixth of seven verses that Herbert speaks of his re-creation when *in age I bud again*. This is a poem of restoration and renewal, but it is also honest about the past's pains. The title, as well as focusing on the returning flowers of spring, may also have in mind the book of Job, where we are reminded that a mortal 'comes up like a flower and withers' (Job 14.2, NRSV). Hurt people can hurt people but, here, Herbert speaks of how he has been led out of such a spiral of unhappiness and resentment and no one is more amazed than he is: *Who would have thought my shrivel'd heart/Could have recover'd greennesse?* When Herbert placed his poems in order, he put this one after his poem 'The Crosse', in the same way as artists often painted small flowers coming up from parched earth, irrigated by Christ's blood at the crucifixion. Christ is the 'flow-er', the one from whom love flows. Reading 'The Flower' always reminds me of a passage from a Christmas Day sermon by John Donne (1953–1962, IV, p. 172):

He can bring thy summer out of winter, though thou
have no spring; though in the ways of fortune, or
understanding, or conscience, thou have been benighted
till now, wintred and frozen, clouded and eclipsed,
damped and benumbed, smothered and stupified till
now, now God comes to thee, not as in the dawning of
the day, not as in the bud of the spring, but as the sun at
noon, to illustrate all shadows, as the sheaves in harvest,
to fill all penuries, all occasions invite His mercies, and
all times are His seasons.

The poem is addressed to God and begins by comparing God's
revisitings to dry souls to flowers that emerge after the win-
ter. He then admits that his heart had gone *quite under ground*
and compares it to flowers that disappear to see their *mother-
root* and, like hibernating animals, *keep house unknown*. It is
a known spiritual truth that dark times, empty and painful
periods of life, can be where necessary distillation takes place.
Our hard full stops are being changed into commas without
us knowing. The cave we fear to enter turns out to be a source
of what we are looking for. It is said that one of the early de-
sert saints used to pray that the word of God would be on our
hearts. He was asked why 'on' and not 'in'? He replied: 'Because
our hearts are so hard it cannot penetrate until the heart breaks
and then it can fall in and be watered and come to fruition.'

Herbert is able to say that this *killing and quickning*
experience is one of God's *wonders*, and then there is the
striking line, *Thy word is all, if we could spell. Spell* is a word
Herbert returns to a lot. It suggests a closer reading of God,
translating understanding into the way we live a life and a
commitment.

The poem ends with Herbert smelling the *dew and rain* and relishing writing poetry again. He notes that we are flowers which *glide* – that is, are impermanent or falling. When we comprehend this, we learn of our dependence on the gardener, who plants us carefully. The last line maybe reveals the lesson his difficulties have taught him: that it is pride which drove Adam and Eve out of the garden and pride still stops us growing in grace. Looking down on things and people all the time stops us seeing what is above. Or, as Carl Jung is often quoted as saying, 'Through pride we are ever deceiving ourselves. But deep down below the surface of the average conscience a still, small voice says to us, something is out of tune.'

Bitter-sweet

Ah my deare angrie Lord,
Since thou dost love, yet strike;
Cast down, yet help afford;
Sure I will do the like.

I will complain, yet praise;
I will bewail, approve:
And all my sowre-sweet days
I will lament, and love.

The short eight lines of this poem take us to the heart of Herbert's relationship with God as expressed in the poems of *The Temple*. Just as a marriage or partnership has its seasons, so, we learn, does life with God. There is the intensity of our first love and the excitement of commitment. There is a honeymoon and periods of mutual learning, and there are later pressures, hurts and disappointments, maybe even betrayal. There is forgiveness or separation, resentment or restoration, and the potential for movement into a deeper, more open-eyed and open-hearted autumnal relationship of a rich mellowness rather than naive aspirations or volatile passion. Relationships cause us to change and they change with us. Our relationship with God is no different. This is what makes faith an adventure.

'Bitter-Sweet' was a name of an apple in Herbert's time and we are transported by this title to Eden where, an apple bitten,

God's children were *cast down, yet help afford* in the life of Christ. The title also reminds us that love itself has sweetness mingled with hurts; grief is often the price we pay for loving. The poem is addressed to God who is both *my deare* and also *angrie*. Love can get angry for good reasons, but is proved in what it does next. Will it work to reconcile and put things right or will it take revenge and withdraw? Herbert suggests here that God is like a parent who has to say 'no' to his or her child so that the child can learn, grow and develop its own discernment as to how the world works. Herbert then, almost like a spoiled child, says that if God is going to love but then make life difficult, *Sure I will do the like*. He can't, of course, do what God does, but he can love and complain. He can moan at God, yet also praise. He can bewail and speak against what God appears to be, but also approve – that is, commend God to others.

The last two lines are telling. They reveal how Herbert's understanding of his relationship grew. In lines 2, 3 and 5 he talks of seeming opposites in terms of *yet*. In the last line, however, the *yet* becomes *and*: *I will lament, and love*. Instead of what appear to be contrary energies somehow battling it out, Herbert now accepts that they will live together. It cannot be any other way. He will *lament* when life is hard or when God appears unfair, ambivalent or absent; at the same time, this will be part of his love. Love is the final word in this relationship. It just takes a few battles to get there. It has been said that God loves us just the way we are, but loves us so much he doesn't want us to stay like that. The changes hurt and can feel cruel. Herbert, though intimate with God in this poem, says that he's not going to pretend otherwise.

'The Lord disciplines those whom he loves', says the letter to the Hebrews (12.6, NRSV). A contemporary of Herbert's, the theologian Richard Sibbes, wrote in a similar vein in his commentary on the second letter of Paul to the Corinthians (1862, p. 221):

> remember that God works by contraries. God will bring us to heaven, but it must be by hell. God will bring us to comfort, but it must be by sense of our own unworthiness. He will forgive our sins, but it must be by sight and sense of our sins. He will bring us to life, but it must be by death. He will bring us to glory, but it must be by shame . . . As in the creation he made all out of nothing, order out of confusion; so in the work of the new creation, he doth so likewise; therefore be not dismayed.

We fear God not because God is angry and vindictive, but because God is real and God's reality works on us to burn off the inauthentic and damaging. We can paddle about in the shallows of religion or we can wake up and see that it is indeed 'a fearful thing to fall into the hands of the living God' (Hebrews 10.31) because we enter the crucible of love.

The Answer

My comforts drop and melt away like snow:
I shake my head, and all the thoughts and ends,
Which my fierce youth did bandie, fall and flow
Like leaves about me; or like summer friends,
Flyes of estates and sunne-shine. But to all,
Who think me eager, hot, and undertaking,
But in my prosecutions slack and small;
As a young exhalation, newly waking,
Scorns his first bed of dirt, and means the sky;
But cooling by the way, grows pursie and slow,
And setling to a cloud, doth live and die
In that dark state of tears: to all, that so
      Show me, and set me, I have one reply,
      Which they that know the rest, know more then I.

This sonnet is not as well known as it should be. One critic has said that it proves Herbert 'read Shakespeare with profit' (Summers, 1954, p. 183) and its form and tone are distinctly recognizable. It is undoubtedly autobiographical and controls within its lines what feels to be more than melancholy. In his poem 'The Flower', Herbert refers to his grief melting away like snow, but here it is comfort that melts. He shakes his head as all the thoughts and intentions that he once had, and was so immersed in and proud of, now, like *leaves*, seem to have fallen to the ground. They are like fair-weather friends, *flyes* who like fortune, *estates*, and sunshine, but buzz off when the freeze sets in.

Herbert then says he is speaking to those who think him eager, adventurous and ready for enterprise but, when it comes to it, they see that he hasn't achieved a great deal, only things *slack and small*. He knows that people will look at him, the one for whom life seemed to offer so much but whose public contribution ended up being so thin, as if he were a vapour formed off damp ground, *a young exhalation*. He rose as if making for the skies but, *cooling by the way*, became swollen and slow like a cloud that turned to rain, *that dark state of tears*. To those who show him this or make his reputation as this, he has one reply. The reply is something of a conundrum, though, and focuses on the word *rest*. Does he mean the remainder of the answer? The rest of his life? The rest of his poems? The rest that comes at the end of life's restlessness? The sonnet is frustrating to the reader as it leads us slowly towards what we feel will be the answer to those who comment on his life, but then leaves us in mystery – not only as to the poem but as to human existence as well!

The sonnet throws up many issues, not least when and how we evaluate our life's worth and whether, in Herbert's faith, the way we discern that worth will be the same as the way God discerns it. It confronts us with the fact that we spend so much time making a life, with energy, drive, anxiety and com-petition motivating us, but when the *leaves* fall and we step back from what we have done and what it has made us, we are at a loss as to what it all means and adds up to. We want to know 'the rest' if it is out there somewhere. We want to have some rest after such tiredness comes over us. Do we care what 'the rest' say about us? What will 'the rest' of our life contain and how might it be different? With just one word, sitting in the middle of the last line, this poem is a scrutiny of the soul that is as relentless as anything Herbert wrote.

On the whole, perhaps religious types prefer answers to questions, but Herbert reveals that faith does its work best by questioning answers. It is a burning acid that tests our certitudes, morality, thoughts and words. It teaches us that the greatest problems in life don't have one answer, but are fundamentally unsolvable. They can't be solved, only outgrown. God is the one who helps us in that growth by teaching us better questions, which always resist easy answers that make honestly complex things dishonestly simple. Faith is the antidote to quick clarity and the commitment to a renewed and patient attention where we are willing to be schooled in the key relationships: those to myself, my neighbour and our God.

The Glance

When first thy sweet and gracious eye
Vouchsaf'd ev'n in the midst of youth and night
To look upon me, who before did lie
            Weltring in sinne;
   I felt a sugred strange delight,
Passing all cordials made by any art,
Bedew, embalme, and overrunne my heart,
          And take it in.

   Since that time many a bitter storm
My soul hath felt, ev'n able to destroy,
Had the malicious and ill-meaning harm
            His swing and sway:
   But still thy sweet originall joy
Sprung from thine eye, did work within my soul,
And surging griefs, when they grew bold, controll,
          And got the day.

   If thy first glance so powerfull be,
A mirth but open'd and seal'd up again;
What wonders shall we feel, when we shall see
            Thy full-ey'd love!
   When thou shalt look us out of pain,
And one aspect of thine spend in delight
More then a thousand sunnes disburse in light,
          In heav'n above.

In his poem 'Love (III)', Herbert finds himself in the presence of God but, because of a sense of shame and unworthiness, he says to God, 'I cannot look on thee.' In this poem 'The Glance', it is, instead, God's look that is the focus. The poem begins with the poet speaking to God and remembering when God's *sweet and gracious eye* first cast itself lovingly on him, looking in on him at night like a devoted parent, looking out and over him through his youth – even though that youth was spent *weltring in sinne*. *Weltring* means wallowing through mud and calls to mind the prodigal son parable, where the son ends up in the pigs' mud while the father is endlessly watching out for him to return home (Luke 15.11–32).

When he sees God's watchful care over him and understands how cherished he is by his maker, Herbert feels a *sugred strange delight*, better than any medicinal drink might bring. This wonder and delight falls on him like dew, anoints and flows over him. His heart is taken in, given shelter and joy, such that life becomes refreshed. The imagery here may have overtones of the baptismal waters, when we are taken into the water and into God's compassion and delight.

Herbert continues to talk about his feelings. Since that time, he says, *many a bitter storm* has come his way and he might even have been destroyed if evil had had its way with full control (*swing and sway*). It didn't, though. The *originall joy* that was placed in his heart by God's tender and loving look never left his soul. So, when *surging griefs* threatened to overwhelm, remembered love controlled and restrained the chaos. Indeed, joy appears to be one of the infallible proofs of God's existence for Herbert.

If, continues Herbert in reflective mood, God's loving glance is so redeeming and restoring to human beings as they make their way through life's difficulties and ride the waves of emotions that make or break them, then imagine what it will be like to be looked on with *full-ey'd love* when we pass from this Earth. St Paul's reflection to the church in Corinth similarly reinforced the truth that here we see God only partially, 'through a glass, darkly', but there will come a day when we see 'face to face' and know God as much as we are already known by him (1 Corinthians 13.12).

The end of the last stanza is particularly beautiful. Herbert looks to the time when God will *look us out of pain*, when being seen and seeing that glance which reveals just how much we are wanted and treasured will dissolve all our hurts and griefs. All pain will disappear as love is fully reciprocated and understood. It will be more glorious and joyful than the light created by a *thousand sunnes*.

Herbert's Christian journey was made with a very strong conflict felt within between the *bitter storm* and *surging griefs* he experienced and the *sweet originall joy* that had centred and shaped his life and his relationship with God. One could argue that the honest tension between these is the source of his poetic creativity and lasting appeal. It is sometimes said that religion is lived by people who are afraid of hell and spirituality is lived by people who have been through hell. His ability to live through the darkness while searching for the light gives him that doubled awareness which furnishes the faithful longing soul and makes it a good and indispensable friend to the rest of us.

Aaron

Holinesse on the head,
Light and perfections on the breast,
Harmonious bells below, raising the dead
To leade them unto life and rest.
        Thus are true Aarons drest.

Profanenesse in my head,
Defects and darknesse in my breast,
A noise of passions ringing me for dead
Unto a place where is no rest.
        Poore priest thus am I drest.

Onely another head
I have, another heart and breast,
Another musick, making live not dead,
Without whom I could have no rest:
        In him I am well drest.

Christ is my onely head,
My alone onely heart and breast,
My onely musick, striking me ev'n dead;
That to the old man I may rest,
        And be in him new drest.

Aaron

So holy in my head,
Perfect and light in my deare breast,
My doctrine tun'd by Christ, (who is not dead,
But lives in me while I do rest)
Come people; Aaron's drest.

As a priest, I always find it important in the vestry before a service to calm my mind somehow and prepare for the privilege of what I am about to do. In some ways, this poem reads like the reflection of a priest in the same situation, a vesting prayer, and one that acknowledges the poverty of the priest's soul and where the inner strength comes from to minister without an overwhelming sense of unworthiness or hypocrisy.

Aaron was the first high priest and, in Exodus 28.2–38, we discover what robes he wore. He wore a mitre, for example, that had 'Holiness to the Lord' written on it, and so this poem, named after Aaron, begins with *Holinesse on the head*, then refers to the breastplate of *light and perfections* he put on and the *bells* that were placed on the hem of his robe. The bells were to stop Aaron dying in the presence of the Holy when he went before the Lord, but Herbert, making Aaron here a prototype for Christ, speaks of them raising the dead *to leade them unto life and rest*. Just as Christ is a high priest, so too priests of Christ are *drest* in their vocation, in the words of John Donne in a poem to a friend just ordained, 'to open life' for people ('To Mr Tilman After He had Taken Orders').

As one of those priests, however, Herbert knows that he is no Aaron. He has *profanenesse* in his head, *defects and darknesse* in his breast and, instead of bells, a cacophony of passions that make him restless and feel as if *he* is the dead one. This is how he, as a priest, is *drest*. Herbert then muses that he has another head, heart and breast in Christ who is his *onely musick*. As Paul tells the Galatians, when we are baptized, we 'put on Christ' (3.27), and Herbert, who we are told always had an eye for tasteful clothes, knows that he is *well drest* in Christ, new and with all his thoughts *tun'd by Christ, (who is not dead,/But lives in me while I do rest)*. Once he reminds himself of this, he is ready again to pick up his vocation and says, *Come people; Aaron's drest*. One of Herbert's contemporaries, Joseph Hall, preached a similar message: 'Happy is it for us . . . if we can have this holy Impresse of God, written not in our foreheads but in our hearts' (Lewalski, 1979, p. 186).

This is a highly structured poem, with a lot of repetition of words that build up new resonances and references as the poem progresses. You feel that, as Herbert reflects, so, like the stringed instrument he is, Christ is tuning him so he gets to the place where he can begin playing life as a priest again. The poet R. S. Thomas writes in one poem that Christ comes to us 'with a sharp song' (1995, p. 215) as it changes the old tunes we plod along to into something more beautiful, intricate, peaceful. At the end of Herbert's poem, you feel the baton is raised to begin afresh.

In and of ourselves, as Herbert knew, our resources are limited and the human material we are made from is fractured, volatile and unique, but full of inheritance as well as potential, as we live out what our past is doing now. It is only by recognizing Christ's compassion towards us, before his call to us, that any of us can dare to use the word 'Christian' to describe ourselves. The same compassion is asked of us, to forgive as we have been forgiven, and only on this foundation can a vocation in life, whether to priesthood or any other life, be embraced. Unawareness is the root of all evil. We must, as Christians, be realistically self-aware and completely trusting that this same self is to become part of God's body language as it lives, moves and has its being in his love.

The Forerunners

The harbingers are come. See, see their mark;
White is their colour, and behold my head.
But must they have my brain? must they dispark
Those sparkling notions, which therein were bred?
     Must dulnesse turn me to a clod?
Yet have they left me, *Thou art still my God.*

Good men ye be, to leave me my best room,
Ev'n all my heart, and what is lodged there:
I passe not, I, what of the rest become,
So *Thou art still my God*, be out of fear.
     He will be pleased with that dittie;
And if I please him, I write fine and wittie.

Farewell sweet phrases, lovely metaphors.
But will ye leave me thus? when ye before
Of stews and brothels onely knew the doores,
Then did I wash you with my tears, and more,
     Brought you to Church well drest and clad:
My God must have my best, ev'n all I had.

Louely enchanting language, sugar-cane,
Hony of roses, whither wilt thou flie?

Hath some fond lover tic'd thee to thy bane?
And wilt thou leave the Church, and love a stie?
    Fie, thou wilt soil thy broider'd coat,
And hurt thy self, and him that sings the note.

Let foolish lovers, if they will love dung,
And canvas, not with arras clothe their shame:
Let follie speak in her own native tongue.
True beautie dwells on high: ours is a flame
    But borrow'd thence to light us thither.
Beautie and beauteous words should go together.

Yet if you go, I passe not; take your way:
For, *Thou art still my God*, is all that ye
Perhaps with more embellishment can say.
Go birds of spring: let winter have his fee,
    Let a bleak palenesse chalk the doore,
So all within be livelier then before.

This is one of Herbert's greatest autobiographical poems. We see the title and expect a poem about prophets or John the Baptist, perhaps, but discover straight away that the forerunners or *harbingers* are actually Herbert's grey hairs that have started to appear. A forerunner was someone who would travel ahead of the royal party and find lodgings for them. Once it had been found, the forerunner would mark the place over the door with white chalk. Herbert, reflecting on his ageing, sees his white hairs as similar marks on him, preparing him for his King.

Meanwhile, he is concerned that, as he gets older, his poetic gifts and sparkling notions may weaken. *Must dulnesse turn me to a clod?* he asks. Will lack of sparkle make him a block-head? Even if it does, continues Herbert, *Thou art still my God.* In the second stanza, he thanks the *harbingers* for not taking over his best room, his heart, and what is lodged there, his faith in Christ. The next two lines may be paraphrased: 'I don't care what happens to the rest; as long as *Thou art still my God,* I will not be afraid.' If his relationship with God is in place, he will be able to continue writing.

He still recognizes that his verse may not be up to what it was, though. He bids farewell to *sweet phrases* and *lovely metaphors,* and is frustrated because, up until Herbert's time, such poetic gifts were used by lewd folk in *stews,* brothels, and wasted on love poetry of dubious quality. Herbert says that he washed poetry with his *tears,* his honest self-appraisals, took it to church properly *drest and clad,* because *My God must have my best, ev'n all I had.*

The fourth verse intoxicates with its sweetness imagery. He asks if enchanting language will now return to its base past. Will it leave the Church and love a pigsty instead? Such disloyalty of redeemed language will end up being bad for it and those who write it. Then, in the fifth stanza, if foolish lovers are intent on wearing rough clothes and not embroidered *arras,* then let them speak in their native tongue because *true beautie dwells on high* and is a borrowed flame to help light our way. *Beautie and beauteous words should go together,* he says.

The last verse is full of resolve. Even if Herbert's poetic skill starts to fail, he won't mind because God is still his God, no matter what and that, ultimately, is all he has been trying to say with his words anyway and may, *perhaps,* still be able to yet. The reservation that lies in the word *perhaps* is palpable. The emblems of youth, *birds of spring,* can fly off and *winter,* the last season of life, can be paid his bill by marking the chalk on his *doore,* because what may be heralded in the end here is not death so much as truth, in his remaining time on Earth and beyond. Herbert, inside, might now be so distilled that he is, and will be, livelier than before.

There is an old saying that just because there is snow on the roof doesn't mean the fire has gone out. As Herbert looks in the mirror and sees his hair, he also sees his life's work, his faith and his increasing frailty, and holds them all up to the God, who is still his, still on the journey, still guiding him to shelter.

Discipline

Throw away thy rod,
Throw away thy wrath:
            Oh my God,
Take the gentle path.

For my heart's desire
Unto thine is bent:
            I aspire
To a full consent.

Not a word or look
I affect to own,
            But by book,
And thy book alone.

Though I fail, I weep:
Though I halt in pace,
            Yet I creep
To the throne of grace.

Then let wrath remove;
Love will do the deed:
            For with love
Stonie hearts will bleed.

Love is swift of foot;
Love's a man of warre,
    And can shoot,
And can hit from farre.

Who can scape his bow?
That which wrought on thee,
    Brought thee low,
Needs must work on me.

Throw away thy rod;
Though man frailties hath,
    Thou art God:
Throw away thy wrath.

It's been said that one of the differences between John Donne and George Herbert is that whereas Donne seems to wonder whether God can make anything of him, whether he will finally be redeemed because he's a very complex and earthy man of the world, Herbert is always assured in the end that he's safe in a friendship with God that nothing can ever threaten. Although Herbert will take on God, often behaving like an adolescent and complaining about the way things are or feel, one always senses that he and his God are together – and for always. It means that Herbert can adopt an audacious or cheeky tone and he appears to banter with God, assured and, frequently, shockingly bold. It's what has always drawn me to him. His belief in love makes him honest and colloquial with his God.

This poem, 'Discipline', is a good example of this approach. Although the form of the poem exemplifies its topic, the taut syllables and balance of emotion making it a disciplined structure, the content is unusually frank. Herbert has decided to ask God not to be angry. He asks God to discipline his people when they fail and fall into evil, but to do it by *the gentle path* and not by the *rod*. In the second stanza he tells God that, personally, he has some self-discipline and aspires to be fully as God wishes him to be, so God really doesn't need to be angry. He isn't being original, he continues, he's just following the Bible as best he can. He fails and weeps at it. He limps his way through a Christian life and tells it as it is: *I creep/To the throne of grace.*

Herbert is convinced that love is a stronger and better way for God to win hearts and minds than wrath. With love, he argues, *stonie hearts will bleed.* If God wants to keep his thunder and lightning techniques, Herbert seems to be saying, then love will do just as well as fiery fury: *Love's a man of warre,/And can shoot.* It was love that made God come down to Earth and now it needs to come down into Herbert again so that his heart can be lifted by it and not diminished or destroyed.

The last stanza nearly repeats the first but, surprisingly, concludes by reminding God that it is humans who have *frailties*, not God, and to be angry would be to demonstrate a weakness and lack of discipline so, once again, God, please, *Throw away thy wrath.* He almost appears to be saying, 'God, you shouldn't feel threatened by us because *Thou art God* and not us! So, keep on loving us and we'll get there eventually, if you stay lovingly patient and encouraging.'

Ultimately, Christians do not fear God because he is angry or vindictive. They fear God because God is real and we are not. Such reality exposes our masks and cover-ups. It exposes our incompleteness and our ability to live lies that we end up believing. Judgement will be liberating because, at last, we will see ourselves as we really are and not how we have constructed our image. When God shows us to ourselves, we hope, with Herbert, that it is done with love, because love is the best transformer and source of change ever known to us.

The Elixer

Teach me, my God and King,
In all things thee to see,
And what I do in any thing,
To do it as for thee:

Not rudely, as a beast,
To runne into an action;
But still to make thee prepossest,
And give it his perfection.

A man that looks on glasse,
On it may stay his eye;
Or if he pleaseth, through it passe,
And then the heav'n espie.

All may of thee partake:
Nothing can be so mean,
Which with his tincture (for thy sake)
Will not grow bright and clean.

A servant with this clause
Makes drudgerie divine:
Who sweeps a room, as for thy laws,
Makes that and th' action fine.

This is the famous stone
That turneth all to gold:
For that which God doth touch and own
Cannot for lesse be told.

This is probably one of Herbert's best-known poems, as it is sung as a hymn because of its clean metrical form. There are a few versions of the poem, owing to Herbert carefully revising it and, if you are used to singing it, you probably won't have come across verse 2 before. To begin with, Herbert called the poem 'Perfection', but then he added the last verse and renamed it 'The Elixer'. Reactions to the poem differ. Some feel that it captures the simplicity and humility of the poet, while others find it a bit clunky and uninspiring.

The poem begins with a prayer similar to that found in Psalm 143: 'Teach me to do thy will; for thou art my God' (143.10). Herbert prays that he may see God in all things and so be able to recognize the sacrament of the present moment. He asks that, whatever he does, he may do it for God and for no other conflicted reason. He doesn't want to be like an unthinking animal that finds itself doing whatever it wants but, rather, *still* – that is, always – allow God to claim what he does and, through God's grace, make it a perfect offering. The word *his* in line 8 means 'its'.

The third verse is the pulse of the poem and is the one verse that remained unchanged through all the revisions. Herbert notes that we can look on the surface of life and things and just leave it there. Or a person, *if he pleaseth*, can look through and beyond them for heaven, God's presence, to be spied from a distance. It is unclear whether *if he pleaseth* refers to the person wanting to have a deeper attention, a changed perspective, or to that attention being possible only if God is pleased with the person. Perhaps, as is often the way in Herbert's poetry, both are intended, as grace does both at the same time.

Herbert continues his prayer: *All may of thee partake.* This surely has eucharistic overtones and may be a better line to have in a service sheet than the many contorted and restrictive rubrics that can often be found at the point when people are invited to the altar or Communion table. *Nothing can be so mean*, so lowly or unrefined, that can't be made acceptable, *bright and clean*, by transforming it with the words *for thy sake*. Herbert uses the alchemical term *tincture*, suggesting a spiritual reality infusing a material one. Even a servant, such as Christ, can transform a demanding and burdensome life by praying *for thy sake*. Herbert's contemporary St François de Sales used the same word that Herbert uses here, *drudgerie*, in his *Introduction to the Devout Life*: 'without devotion, repose is but idleness, and labour is but drudgerie' (de Sales, 1614, p. 163). If you clean a room as if it were for God's comfort, continues the poet, it makes both the business of cleaning and the room itself fine or uncommonly admirable.

For thy sake is the clause that changes everything because it sees life as a divine gift that we must respond to in all our words and behaviour. Like the philosopher's stone, known as the elixer, which was thought to transform base metal into gold, the words *for thy sake* are a spiritual alchemy, guaranteeing a new reality for us. If God *doth touch* – that is, checks like a touchstone – the worth of the gold, then nothing will ever make us *lesse* than that which he values above everything else.

The poet Seamus Heaney once said in a radio programme that his first poems were trying to write like stained glass, but he later wanted to write like window glass. The spiritual life has its comparisons. To be able to seek God transparently, to make God our ultimate end in all we do, in the simple but taxing things of everyday life, is the Christian vocation. One of Herbert's proverbs may help us into this poem, and into the day that lies ahead for us: 'Love makes one fitt for any work' (1640, p. 646).

A Wreath

A wreathed garland of deserved praise,
Of praise deserved, unto thee I give,
I give to thee, who knowest all my wayes,
My crooked winding wayes, wherein I live,
Wherein I die, not live; for life is straight,
Straight as a line, and ever tends to thee,
To thee, who art more farre above deceit,
Then deceit seems above simplicitie.
Give me simplicitie, that I may live,
So live and like, that I may know thy wayes,
Know them and practise them: then shall I give
For this poore wreath, give thee a crown of praise.

In St Paul's first letter to the Corinthians (9.25) he makes a distinction between a perishable wreath of honour that runners compete to win, made of leaves or flowers, and the imperishable wreath that awaits those who don't live their lives aimlessly but seek to remain faithful to the gospel of Christ. Herbert, similarly, compares the reality of his own *poore wreath* with the *crown of praise* that he longs to offer Christ in his life – for Christ deserves nothing less.

The form of the poem is suitably wreath-like. It is circular, in the sense that the end of each line is picked up by the next, the words intertwining together and so weaving a poem where the very last line ties up with the first. This interlacing is not perfectly neat, as indeed wreaths aren't, and so poorly compares with the perfect circle of the crown worn by the one whom Herbert calls in the poem 'Praise (II)' 'King of Glorie, King of Peace'.

The syntax of the first line means one could think either that the subject is a wreath of praise glorifying God as God deserves to be glorified or Herbert is referring to a wreath which is so beautiful, it is deservedly praised. This is a clever insight that Herbert places in view straight away. Whenever we start talking about how well we praise God or how well we are living the Christian life or serving our neighbour and so on, we begin to sound, at best, self-focused or, at worst, self-righteous. It is a very difficult thing to prise off our own crowns and hand them over for good. Herbert knows this and is more than aware that God also *knowest all my wayes*. This poem is a prayer and, as such, Herbert does not want to avoid the ambiguities and contradictions of the Christian life he is trying to live. Even his piety, admits the poet, is caught up in his *crooked winding wayes*.

By using the phrase *winding wayes*, Herbert seems to be making some comparison of a selfish life to the wreath itself, making it an existence of fragmented circularity and one that cannot reach beyond itself. The snake in the garden of Eden, of course, was also winding in form as he tempted human beings to go their own way. Herbert is conscious that his *crooked winding wayes* in life can make him cleverly evasive of the path he knows to be right.

By not having the willpower to be undeviating, Herbert says that his life is really a sort of death and this will stay the case if he doesn't finally commit to a way of living that seriously and purposefully pursues the holiness of God. This way is *straight* in that it is a road to be kept to, and, *straight* sounding the same as 'strait', we are reminded that it is narrow and not always as all-encompassing as we sometimes like to imagine.

Herbert speaks to God as the one who is *farre above deceit*. Herbert knows his own capacity for deviousness and denial. He knows that an empty person is full of himself. He longs for the *simplicitie* of God that would distil him and enable him to live a life worthy of the name and a life that is praising of God in the way it is being lived. He yearns not only to *know* God's ways but also to *practise them*. All the way through this poem, the two words *live* and *give* rhyme in a teasing harmony. Life has been given to the poet and what he gives to God in return is *poore* in comparison, unless it is in tune with the kingdom in which God alone, and not the world's dishonesty, wears the crown.

Heaven

O who will show me those delights on high?
>   *Echo.*   *I.*

Thou Echo, thou art mortall, all men know.
>   *Echo.*   *No.*

Wert thou not born among the trees and leaves?
>   *Echo.*   *Leaves.*

And are there any leaves, that still abide?
>   *Echo.*   *Bide.*

What leaves are they? impart the matter wholly.
>   *Echo.*   *Holy.*

Are holy leaves the Echo then of blisse?
>   *Echo.*   *Yes.*

Then tell me, what is that supreme delight?
>   *Echo.*   *Light.*

Light to the minde: what shall the will enjoy?
>   *Echo.*   *Joy.*

But are there cares and businesse with the pleasure?
>   *Echo.*   *Leisure.*

Light, joy, and leisure; but shall they persever?
>   *Echo.*   *Ever.*

In Greek mythology, Echo fell in love with Narcissus, but her love was never returned and she faded away in sorrow until all that was left was her disembodied voice. In this poem, Echo's voice is present, but she appears to be a personification of some heavenly messenger or maybe of the Bible. Herbert's contemporary John Donne preached a sermon in 1624 in which he said that 'The Scriptures are Gods Voyce; The Church is his Echo; a redoubling, a repeating of some particular syllables, and accents of the same voice' (1953–1962, VI, 11). It is clear that this excellent example of an echo poem, and such poems were popular in Herbert's day and well before, is a metaphor for our communication with God, as well as a chamber in which we catch the faint, intimate but partial sounds of truth as faith perceives it.

When Herbert placed his poems in order, he ensured that this one was the penultimate poem, followed only by 'Love (III)', but preceded by 'Judgement'. He called it 'Heaven', the place where God is. He didn't write a poem on hell. Although heaven can be thought of as some faraway land where the redeemed go to be with God, the heaven that Herbert seems to be thinking of consists of those places where God is on this Earth and in our lives. We pray in the Lord's Prayer that God's will be done 'on earth as it is in heaven' (Matthew 6.10, NRSV) but it is not only God's will that must be celebrated in both realms but God's presence too.

The poem begins with a question as to who will reveal something to the poet about those delights on high. An authoritative *I* replies. The poet says Echo is mortal and, therefore, won't know much about eternity, but this Echo is not that of the classical myth and counters his argument. Ovid's Echo was a wood nymph and was *born among the trees and leaves*, but, again, this Echo is a different being who suggests that *leaves* are her natural landscape but they are the *leaves* of a book – the Bible. These are the *leaves* that still *abide*, continually last. The speaker wants to know more. What sort of leaves are they? *Holy* comes the reply. He sees then that these *leaves* are themselves the echo of heaven.

Echo continues to reveal that the *supreme delight* is *light* and that the psalmist was right when praying 'in thy presence is fulness of joy' (Psalm 16.11). Joy is the currency of God's dwelling place, not *cares and businesse*. The poem ends wanting a clarification. Heaven is a place of light, joy and leisure – but always, without any end? Echo says *Ever*, bringing to mind the end of the Lord's Prayer this time – 'for ever and ever'. Heaven is not a place of existence, but of life eternal. The poet's uncertainties are resolved by that word *ever* at the end. One critic, Helen Vendler, sums up the end of the poem by reflecting, 'Surely the doctrine of final perseverance, by which transient grace turns to permanent glory, deserves to have the word "ever" embodied in it' (1975, pp. 222–9).

I am drawn to the idea that the Scriptures and the Church's teaching are dimmed but discernible echoes, not the full or permanent voice, of God. Echoes beguile, bewilder, intrigue and invite us to keep listening because more may be on its way and is liable to be missed. Echoes are an incomplete and imperfect repetition of the true. One cannot confuse them as being identical and yet they are inseparably related. What this poem also teaches us again is that, to understand something of heaven, of God's presence, you must have a humble mind that can question and receive hints and guesses, rather than full answers, with joyful gratitude and a renewed spirit of adventure.

Love (III)

Love bade me welcome: yet my soul drew back,
          Guiltie of dust and sinne.
But quick-ey'd Love, observing me grow slack
          From my first entrance in,
Drew nearer to me, sweetly questioning,
          If I lack'd any thing.

A guest, I answer'd, worthy to be here:
          Love said, you shall be he.
I the unkinde, ungratefull? Ah my deare,
          I cannot look on thee.
Love took my hand, and smiling did reply,
          Who made the eyes but I?

Truth Lord, but I have marr'd them: let my shame
          Go where it doth deserve.
And know you not, sayes Love, who bore the blame?
          My deare, then I will serve.
You must sit down, sayes Love, and taste my meat:
          So I did sit and eat.

From the very first line of Herbert's poem, we hear the bounce and eagerness of Love in the short syllables of *Love bade me welcome* and the contrast with the long and heavy syllables of *my soul drew back*. Similarly, *quick-ey'd Love* is sprightly in comparison to *grow slack*. The tone of the dialogue is set straight away and certain biblical passages come to mind, including the parable of the wedding feast, when the guests fail to turn up in Matthew 22.1–14, and Psalm 23.5 and Luke 12.37, where God serves at a table for guests who consider themselves undeserving. In Luke's telling of Christ's parable of the feast to which the invited guests don't come, we read that 'A certain man made a great supper, and bade many' (Luke 14.16). Here, it is Love that *bade* the poet welcome.

A universal appeal to the poem is created by Herbert using the word *Love* instead of God or Christ, making the person of faith recall that love is the only metaphor for God which should be pursued relentlessly. It also helps the doubter to get beyond the loaded word 'God' that may have so many shadows attached to it because of the way it can be used abusively. For the poet Edwin Muir, brought up in a very rigorous Presbyterianism, God was 'three angry letters in a little black book' (1989, p. 228). Here, though, Love draws *nearer*. Love sees how the man is pulling away. Love also *sweetly* questions him, asking three questions in the poem, while the man asks only one. At a time when many see religion as a project to answer questions, this is helpfully corrective. Love, instead of answering questions, questions our answers.

The poet calls himself unworthy, *unkinde, ungratefull.* He cannot look Love in the eye. He asks that *my shame/Go where it doth deserve.* Guilt is 'I have done something wrong'. Shame is deeper and more paralysing: shame is 'I am something wrong'. Too often religion has contributed to shame in people and here is a beautiful image of God as Love, moving to heal that shame and reassure the poet that, regardless of what others may say or do, God loves him for who he is. Love reaches out and touches him, takes him by the *hand* and then cracks a pun: *Who made the eyes but I?* This is God as friend, not despot. His eyes are sensitive and full of tenderness.

Love is smiling as he speaks and reminds the poet that Love has borne all the blame already. The man is *guiltie of dust and sinne* and the dust from humanity's long road since its divine creation lies heavy on us, but just as Simon Peter protested his unworthiness and Christ washed his feet in reply, so here Love prepares a meal and asks the guest to stop beating himself up and to eat and enjoy what is set before him. Love has carried the blame for Herbert's unworthiness and the only thing asked of him now is that he sits down and enjoys nourishment. The master becomes the servant.

The poem ends with six very short, equally stressed words conveying a poignant surrender to the words and loving body language of God that have brought a peace to his inner conflicts against all the odds: *So I did sit and eat.* The last lines of a Herbert poem so often transform, even subvert, everything that has gone before them. You sense in them that God might do the same to a human life as it draws to its close, such is the power of his love.

So many voices today come at us from every side, telling us that we are small, fat, ugly, stupid, poor and not of any value unless we dance to the tune of the culture's advertisers. We internalize these voices, believing ourselves to be valueless, but often lash out at others to hide it. Here we find the gospel encapsulated in a few intimately charged lines: don't listen to the noisy bullying voices because only one matters – the voice that comes from heaven telling you who you really are, that you are loved and wanted and for always. The gospel asks us to live up to this voice and not to live down to the others. The last line, in a typical Herbert monosyllabic resolution, shows us that the banquet begins when the man finally listens to Love and sits with him, no doubt to continue a conversation in which they can now, at last, look into each other's eyes.

Most of us think there is something that God must hate about us. Herbert, in this magnificent poem, shows that, quite the contrary, God looks at us and loves and then holds out his hand, smiling. When Herbert placed his poems together for his friend to look at, he was careful as to the order in which he placed them. He placed this poem right at the end. The message was clear: for the person of faith, *Love* must always be the last word.

References

Auden, W. H., *Herbert: Poems selected by W. H. Auden* (London: Penguin, 1973), pp. 7 and 8.

St Augustine, *On Christian Doctrine*, I, 36, 40.

St Augustine, Tractate 4, Tractates on the First Epistle of John, John W. Rettig (trans.), in *The Fathers of the Church*, Volume 92 (Washington, DC: Catholic University of America Press, 1995), p. 179.

Baxter, Richard, *Poetical Fragments* (London, 1681), A7v.

Benet, Diana, *Secretary of Praise: The poetic vocation of George Herbert* (Columbia, SC: University of Missouri Press, 1984), p. 136.

Bloch, Chana, *Spelling the Word: George Herbert and the Bible* (Berkeley, CA: University of California Press, 1985), p. 139.

Bourke, Vernon J. (ed.), *The Essential Augustine* (Indianapolis, IN: Hackett, 1974), p. 123.

Buber, Martin, *Eclipse of God* (New York: Harper & Row, 1957).

Burnaby, John, *Amor Dei: A study of the religion of St Augustine* (Eugene, OR: Wipf & Stock, 2007), p. 96.

Coleridge, S. T., *Biographia Literaria* (London, 1817), Nigel Leask (ed.) (London: Everyman, 1997), p. xix.

Coleridge, S. T., 'Letter to Lady Beaumont, 18 March 1826', in *Memorials of Coleorton: Being letters from Coleridge, Wordsworth and his sister, Southey, and Sir Walter Scott to Sir George and Lady Beaumont of Coleorton, Leicestershire, 1803–1834*, Vol. II, William A. Knight (ed.) (Edinburgh: D. Douglas, 1887), pp. 248–9.

References

Donne, John, *The Divine Poems*, Helen Gardner (ed.) (Oxford: Clarendon Press, 1952), pp. 32 and 50.

Donne, John (Evelyn M. Simpson and George R. Potter, eds), *The Sermons of John Donne* (10 volumes) (Berkeley, CA: University of California Press, 1953–1962) III, 5; IV, 172; VI, 11.

Eliot, T. S., *George Herbert* (London: Longmans, Green & Co., 1962), p. 33.

Fuller, Thomas, *Joseph's Party-Coloured Coat* (London, 1640), p. 69.

Halewood, William H., *The Poetry of Grace: Reformation themes and structures in English seventeenth-century poetry* (Newhaven, CT: Yale University Press, 1970), p. 90.

Herbert, Edward (Will H. Dircks, ed.), *The Autobiography of Edward, Lord Herbert of Cherbury* (London: Walter Scott, 1888), p. 12.

Herbert, George, *A Priest to the Temple, or, The Country Parson, his Character and Rule of Holy Life* in *The Complete English Poems*, John Tobin (ed.) (London: Penguin, 1991), pp. 204 and 205.

Herbert, George, *Outlandish Proverbs* (London, 1640), p. 646.

Knights, L. C., *Explorations*, (London: Chatto & Windus, 1946), p. 141.

Larkin, Philip (Archie Burnett, ed.), 'Days', *The Complete Poems* (London: Faber & Faber, 2012), p. 60.

Lewalski, B. K., *Protestant Poetics and the Seventeenth-century Religious Lyric* (Princeton, NJ: Princeton University Press, 1979), p. 186.

MacNeice, Louis, *Varieties of Parables* (Cambridge: Cambridge University Press, 1965), pp. 8 and 46.

Milton, John, *Paradise Lost* (London: Penguin, 2003), iv 256.

References

Muir, Edwin, *Collected Poems* (London: Faber & Faber, 1989), p. 228.

Nuttall, A. D., *Overheard by God: Fiction and prayer in Herbert, Milton, Dante and St John* (London: Methuen, 1980), p. 34.

Patrides, C. A. (ed.), *George Herbert: The critical heritage* (Abingdon: Routledge, 1983), pp. 166–73.

Sales, François de, *Introduction to the Devout Life* (3rd edn) (Rouen, 1614), p. 163.

Sibbes, Richard (Alexander Balloch Grosart, ed.), *The Complete Works of Richard Sibbes, Volume III: Containing a Commentary on the First Chapter of the Second Epistle to the Corinthians* (Edinburgh: James Nichol, 1862), p. 221.

Skulsky, Harold, 'The Fellowship of the Mystery: Emergent and exploratory metaphor in Vaughan', *Studies in English Literature, 1500–1900*, Winter 1987, 27(1), pp. 89–107.

Stein, Arnold, *George Herbert's Lyrics* (Baltimore, MD: Johns Hopkins University Press, 1968), p. 19.

Summers, Joseph H., *George Herbert: His religion and art* (London: Chatto & Windus, 1954), pp. 61 and 183.

Thomas, R. S., *Collected Poems 1945–1990* (London: Phoenix, 1995), pp. 104 and 215.

Tutu, Desmond, *An African Prayer Book* (London: Image, 2006).

Veith, Gene Edward, Jr, *Reformation Spirituality: The religion of George Herbert* (London: Associated University Presses, 1985), p. 195.

Vendler, Helen, *The Poetry of George Herbert* (Cambridge, MA: Harvard University Press, 1975), pp. 184 and 222–9.

Vendler, Helen, *Invisible Listeners: Lyric intimacy in Herbert, Whitman, and Ashbery* (Princeton, NJ: Princeton University Press, 2005), p. 9.

References

Walton, Izaak, *The Life of Mr George Herbert* (London, 1670), reprinted in *George Herbert: The complete English works*, Ann Pasternak Slater (ed.) (London: Everyman, 1995), pp. 338–85.

Recommended reading

Bloch, Chana, *Spelling the Word: George Herbert and the Bible* (Berkeley, CA: University of California Press, 1985).

Drury, John, *Music at Midnight: The life and poetry of George Herbert* (London: Penguin, 2013).

Falloon, Jane, *Heart in Pilgrimage: A study of George Herbert* (Bloomington, IN: AuthorHouse, 2007).

Hodgkins, Christopher, *Authority, Church and Society in George Herbert: Return to the middle way* (Columbia, SC: University of Missouri Press, 1993).

Rickey, Mary Ellen, *Utmost Art: Complexity in the verse of George Herbert* (Lexington, KY: University of Kentucky Press, 1966).

Strier, Richard, *Love Unknown: Theology and experience in George Herbert's poetry* (Chicago, IL: University of Chicago Press, 1983).

Summers, Joseph H., *George Herbert: His religion and art* (London: Chatto & Windus, 1954).

Tuve, Rosemond, *A Reading of George Herbert* (Chicago, IL: University of Chicago Press, 1952).

Vendler, Helen, *The Poetry of George Herbert* (Cambridge, MA: Harvard University Press, 1975).

Wilcox, Helen (ed.), *The English Poems of George Herbert* (Cambridge: Cambridge University Press, 2007).